Comments

"As an original member of the TWGEYEE I was excited to read Paul and Ken's follow-up publication to the eyewitness guide. In particular, I was very pleased to see they included the chapter on The Cognitive Interview. I have always felt interview skills for the investigator were paramount in the eyewitness identification process. After all if we are dealing with a process we know is flawed wouldn't we do everything possible to improve it? Research has proven that first responders and investigators receive very little training in interviewing the cooperating witness. I firmly believe that not only has flawed eyewitness testimony led to wrongful convictions, but to a lesser degree poor investigative interview skills have also contributed.

Eyewitness testimony has been described as more compelling in some cases than is DNA or physical evidence. Shouldn't evidence as critical as eyewitness testimony be treated as cautiously as trace evidence? How do we do this? The answer is simple the sequential line up with blind administration. Many agencies that try to convert to the sequential process receive push back, stating the process adds a second investigator into the process thus creating additional court time. This is simply not the case. When my agency converted to the process in 2009 we trained over 200 investigators on the process. One reason for our success was the fact we educated our personnel and prosecutors on the process. With this new and better process an area for defense suppression was taken away, which actually cut down on needless suppression hearings."

"The bottom line is the sequential lineup process is a better more reliable process, easily taught and administered and should be adopted by every law enforcement agency in the nation. The original guide just scratched the surface. This book tells the rest of the story."

Major J.R. Burton, Hillsborough County Sheriff's Office Tampa, Florida

"This a clear, careful, readable, book that brings together the best of the street, the lab, and the courtroom to make sure that in eyewitness cases the guilty get convicted and the innocent don't--- a very valuable contribution for anyone who cares about doing good work in the justice system." *James Doyle, Attorney at Law Carney & Bassil, Boston, MA*
-Visiting Fellow, National Institute of Justice
-Director, Center for Modern Forensic Practice, John Jay College of Criminal Justice
-Head, Public Defender Division, Massachusetts Committee for Public Counsel Services
-Author: "True Witness: Cops, Courts, Science and the Battle Against Misidentification."

"A valuable guide for law enforcement professionals at all levels. This thorough, concise and reader friendly guide is brought to life by our real-life experiences. Should be required reading for both newly promoted and veteran detectives." *Sgt. David Ryan (ret.), Detective Division, Chicago Police Department*

"This book is just like the author's day long Eyewitness Evidence class, without the jokes. An easy book to read. It has lots of great information." *LGC, Chicago, Illinois*

"Excellent! I thought that it was terrific, very clear and well organized. The book is packed with great and practical suggestions." *Susan A. Bandes, Professor of Law and Dean's Distinguished Scholar, University of Miami Law School*

"This book should be in every investigator's desk drawer and referred to frequently. We provide tools and knowledge to ensure that eyewitness evidence is accurate and stands up to the scrutiny of today's criminal and civil trials." *Officer Daniel Donoghue Sr., Willow Springs, Illinois Police Department*

This document is not intended to create, does not create, and may not be relied upon to create any rights, substantive or procedural, enforceable at law by any party in any criminal or civil proceeding.

The opinions or points of view expressed within are those of the authors and do not constitute any official position by any department, law enforcement or criminal justice agency. In the event that procedures, other than those recommended in this publication are employed, it does not necessarily mean that the resulting identification is wrong or tainted in any way.

November 2011

Eyewitness testimony runs the risk of being unreliable, which causes more miscarriages of justice than any other method of proof.

From the *Evidence Handbook, 4th Edition* the Traffic Institute, Northwestern University 1980

(t)he vagaries of eyewitness identification are well-known; the annals of criminal law are rife with instances of eyewitness misidentification

United States Supreme Court, U.S. v Wade, 388 U.S. 218, 228 (1967)

There is almost nothing more convincing than a live human being who takes the stand, points a finger at the defendant and says "That's the one."

United States Supreme Court, Watkins v. Sowders, 449 U.S. 341, 352 (1981)

Table of Contents

Preface

This is a sequel to the October 1999 U.S. Department of Justice, Office of Justice Programs, National Institute of Justice publication *Eyewitness Evidence, a Guide for Law Enforcement.*[1]

We were planning panel members (from 1998 to 2002) of the U.S. Department of Justice, National Institute of Justice, Technical Working Group for Eyewitness Evidence (TWGEYEE),[2] the developers and producers of the original eyewitness Guide and the subsequent September 2003 Eyewitness Evidence training manual.[3]

This book is in response to the many requests the authors have received from law enforcement officials, public defenders, defense attorneys, legislators and professors over the past eleven plus years asking for an update and additional information regarding their experiences with eyewitness evidence.

This book is also an answer to the original TWGEYEE members who had hoped to continue their ground breaking work with a follow up publication from the United States Department of Justice to their original eyewitness Guide. We feel, very strongly, that the original publication left many questions unanswered, especially concerning the use and benefit of sequential and blind identification procedures. The omissions at that time were intentional. The law enforcement officer members felt at the time of the original publication that further research, under field conditions, were required to secure widespread acceptance of the recommended procedures. We have taken many of the procedural steps from the NIJ Guide that relate to the sequential double blind identification procedure and included them within.

---

[1] Available at : http://www.ncjrs.gov/app/publications/abstract.aspx?ID'17824

[2] A group of 34 law enforcement professionals, legal practitioners and researchers

[3] Eyewitness Evidence, a Trainers Manual for Law Enforcement available at www.ncjrs.gov/app/publications/abstract.aspx?ID'188678

To date, there has not been substantial research regarding the use of live lineups, or of live "confirmation" identification procedures (i.e.; live lineup at some time in the future after a photo identification has been used to obtain probable cause), which are employed by some of the country's largest law enforcement agencies. We intend to address those procedures and some of the other questions that remain foremost in our minds in this publication.

We admit that this book is neither a research report nor a scholarly document. This book is designed to be a summary of the continuing problems facing the criminal justice system regarding eyewitness evidence based on our experiences and points of view. We have, however, included and quoted relevant research when available and provided a list of additional reading materials. Where our opinions differ, we have so noted.

We want to be clear that it is our opinion and experience that the vast majority of the tens of thousands of eyewitness identifications every year are conducted by well meaning, dedicated professionals who truly desire to faithfully serve the citizens within their respective jurisdictions. The great majority of the eyewitness identifications they obtain is correct and is usually substantiated by other forms evidence. We do, however, feel that with two hundred eighty (280) overturned criminal convictions using DNA technology alone, something must be wrong. Additionally, one University of Michigan study indicates that in the fifteen years between 1989 and 2003 there were three hundred and twenty-eight (328) persons exonerated and freed from prison (four posthumously after they died in prison), due to faulty eyewitness identifications, clearly suggesting that the police identification procedures are deficient.

We also recognize and acknowledge that DNA evidence is not readily available in the vast majority of criminal cases that make their way to our nation's criminal courts. DNA evidence is usually only available or sought in only the most heinous crimes; rapes and homicides. We are all too aware that these types of crimes make up a very small minority of the overall crime statistics. With that in mind, we wonder how many innocent persons are in our jails and penitentiaries. Professor Samuel Gross in his University of Michigan study made this statement, "Could it be that false convictions in capital cases really are no more common than in other cases?" If that were the whole story it would mean that if we reviewed prison sentences with the same level of care that we devote to death sentences, there would have been more than 29,000 non-death row exonerations in the past fifteen years rather than the 280 exonerations that have occurred, including more than 3,700 exonerations in non-capital murder cases alone.[4]

Is it possible that eyewitness evidence is a house of cards, positioned to collapse under the weight of recent scrutiny? Is eyewitness evidence relied on or given too much credibility by prosecutors and our court? Is eyewitness evidence subject to unintentional manipulation? Would better physical evidence awareness and collection assist in answering these questions? Although eyewitness accounts and human memory have been and currently are being scrutinized as a result of the many exonerations over the last two plus decades we do not dismiss the fact that eyewitness accounts can be very valuable to law enforcement. However, those of us in law enforcement must do our investigative due diligence when examining this form of evidence. In the upcoming chapters we will offer easy but significant cost effective and what is more important, judicial improvements when conducting eyewitness identification procedures.

While we acknowledge the cost related budget problems with any forensic testing, how much lower would the true cost be to society if more crimes are solved and there were no civil judgments assessed on governments from wrongful convictions? Consider, if you will, what the cost of crime in our society is and

---

[4] Samuel R. Gross, Kristen Jacoby, Daniel J. Matheson, Nicholas Montgomery & Sujatata Patil, *Exonerations in the United States 1989 through 2003*, The Journal of Criminal Law & Criminology, Vol. 95 No. 2, 2005, Northwestern University of Law, School of Law. Available at: http://www.mindfully.org/Reform/2004/PrisonExonerationsGross19apr04.htm

what the cost is of leaving the real offender at large to commit more crimes while an innocent man sits in the penitentiary.

For many years, we have been advocates of the new procedures and have conducted speaking engagements and instructional courses around the country promoting the eyewitness evidence reforms identified within the DOJ publication; *Eyewitness Evidence: A Guide for Law Enforcement.* We have adjusted our position and advocated for further changes that go beyond what the DOJ publication offers. We strongly suggest and advocate that law enforcement agencies reform their eyewitness identification procedures to mandate the sequential presentation of individuals in live lineups or photographs contained within arrays rather than the traditional simultaneous process.

Also, we believe strongly that the double blind administrator be mandated by the law enforcement community as well. The social science research and DNA technology has taught us all in the criminal justice system that our current eyewitness identification practices are flawed. The outline contained within the original guide is a very good start for an agency that may be apprehensive about making changes to their current practices. However, those procedures are still not enough to prevent the injustices that are continuing to occur.

Sgt. Paul B. Carroll (retired)
Detective Division
Chicago, Illinois Police Department
Homosassa Springs, Florida
www.paulbcarroll.com
sgtpcret@aol.com

Capt. Kenneth A. Patenaude (retired)
Northampton, Massachusetts Police Department
Easthampton, Massachusetts
kpnpd51@aol.com

Introduction

The importance of eyewitness identification cannot be overstated as it has been the primary piece of evidence used in trials across the country for over a century. What is more compelling to a jury than a victim or a witness pointing to the defendant and telling all those present that the individual sitting at the defense table committed the crime? As stated earlier, law enforcement has been using some form or process of presenting suspects to victims and witnesses for the purpose of identifying the guilty party and has had a great deal of success for many decades. However, since the advent of DNA technology in the late 1980s, there have been 280 exonerations to date of persons previously convicted in criminal court. These persons have been adjudged as innocent.

Professor Hugo Munsterberg in 1907 wrote a series of articles titled, "On the Witness Stand" detailing his findings and concerns regarding the errors of eyewitnesses. In *Commonwealth v. Andrews*, a Massachusetts case of forgery involving 17 eyewitnesses incorrectly identifying Andrews as the forger of many checks. After Andrews was incarcerated the actual check forger continued his illegal campaign. He was eventually caught and confessed to the crimes. Andrews was exonerated.

Professor Edwin Borchard in 1932 wrote a book titled, *Convicting the Innocent*, which identified his studies into the fallibility of human memory as it pertained to the criminal justice system. There are many publications and cases that have been attempting to educate the criminal justice system about the ills of human memory as it pertains to identifying individuals that have committed crimes.

What is important to us in the criminal justice community is the fact that we understand that our past practices may have led to wrongful convictions and that there are improved methods to employ to prevent further injustices. A dual injustice occurs when we convict an innocent person while the guilty person is still free to commit more crimes against your community. The criminal justice system is an adversarial one where the prosecution is responsible for winning the case, but they are also responsible for being the ministers of justice. The District Attorney or States Attorney serves all the people, not just the victims or the innocent.

There are those times when these two responsibilities will clash where winning may result in an innocent person going to prison. Scrutiny must occur across the spectrum and on all levels of criminal investigations so that further injustices may be reduced or avoided.

If your law enforcement agency has not added an eyewitness identification policy and training program that, at the very least, follows the Department of Justice publication titled, *Eyewitness Evidence: A Guide for Law Enforcement*, now is the time to make those changes. We offer what we believe to be improved methods that go beyond what is outlined in that Department of Justice Guide. These improved methods come from what researchers originally told us back in 1998, current research and what current practitioners of those methods have told us today work best.

We strongly believe that the identification method that should be employed today is to conduct a sequential double blind lineup and/or photo array. This method of identifying perpetrators represents the best practice for law enforcement to reduce the chances of further misidentifications and wrongful convictions.

The U.S. Department of Justice (DOJ), Office of Justice Programs (OJP), National Institute of Justice (NIJ) continued its mandate from former U.S. Attorney General Janet Reno and her successor, U.S. Attorney General John Ashcroft in 2001. The Justice Department funded the additional efforts of TWGEYEE members in its educational efforts and subsequently published (in

September 2003) *Eyewitness Evidence, A Trainers Guide for Law Enforcement* (Trainers Guide) after numerous meetings by TWGEYEE members. The trainers guide publication followed the original Guide exactly; however, the Trainers Guide provided a detailed explanation for every item and recommendation in the Guide. The trainer's guide was designed in the format of a lesson plan, complete with a PowerPoint presentation. TWGEYEE members felt these explanations would assist the police trainers to fully understand the reasoning behind the material.

After several meetings and discussions, it was decided to publish the eyewitness evidence training guide in modules. TWGEYEE members felt that when published in this manner, police academies and police trainers could cut and paste, taking sections of the guide to supplement their existing training programs in eyewitness evidence.

To our dismay, we soon found that very few police training academies or police trainers had any form of eyewitness evidence training. Most officers, it seems, learned about show-ups, lineups and other identification procedures from a more senior officer when the occasion would arise.

One change that stands out to us is the actual medium used in non-live identification procedures. Strange as it seems to those of us with some longevity in law enforcement, actual photographs have been replaced (very quickly it turned out) with digital images. When the Technical Working Group for Eyewitness Evidence (TWGEYEE) began work on *Eyewitness Evidence, a Guide for Law Enforcement* (the Guide) photographs and mug books were the norm. The use of computer generated images of suspects and those who had been arrested was in its infancy. We did not anticipate how quickly digital technology would be integrated into every day police software programs, thus slowly eliminating the need for mug books. When we lecture around the country about the importance and benefits of identification procedure instructions, sequential and double blind procedures, evidently a whole generation of law enforcement personnel is unaware of the term or use of the mug book. This seems to us to be the same as our children believing that the only way to make popcorn is in a microwave oven. Our children have no idea what Jiffy Pop or homemade (made in a pot on a stove top with real melted butter) popcorn really is.

Many jurisdictions have adopted the procedures enumerated in the original Guide. Some departments went the extra steps and adopted sequential and double blind procedures.

On April 18, 2001, Attorney General John J. Farmer, Jr., of New Jersey, issued the Attorney General "Guidelines for Preparing and Conducting Photo and Live Identification Procedures." [5] Those guidelines specifically decreed that all law enforcement agencies within the state of New Jersey, whenever possible, would follow the instructions in the Guide for all identification procedures. This change was to occur within one hundred eighty (180) days.[6] Most law enforcement professionals can only imagine the resistance and fears of doom that were heard from the New Jersey officers.

While it may seem strange to most criminal justice professionals that the State Attorney General could order all law enforcement agencies to adopt a policy, New Jersey gives its Attorney General that complete and widespread authority. It was an appropriate change to make by that the AG's office as New Jersey was facing real challenges from its Appellate and Supreme Courts. There were overturned convictions and profiling issues making headlines almost daily and a drastic step forward was required. Mr. Farmer had the foresight to be the right man at the right time. More than a decade after adopting the new procedures, "The sky did not fall in" according to New Jersey Assistant Attorney General Lori Linski, Indeed in a 2011 decision, the New Jersey Supreme Court adopted the changes ordered by the Attorney

---

[5]   Available at: http://www.state.nj.us/lps/dcj/agguide/photoid.pdf

[6] Note that in New Jersey, the Attorney General is the chief law enforcement official within the state and has authority over all law enforcement functions throughout the State of New Jersey.

General a decade earlier.[7]

The law enforcement community, as a whole, seems resistant to change (any change). The change to sequential identification procedures from simultaneous procedures and that the identification procedures be administered by someone other than the lead investigator (double blind) was entirely too extreme. After all, we were getting convictions with the old simultaneous identification procedures, weren't we? So why should we change now? What the heck was the Attorney General thinking?

Of course there are those in the criminal justice system that felt making such a drastic change would cause identifications to plummet, arrest numbers to decrease and convictions would be impossible to obtain and eventually, the sky would fall. Our own research has revealed that some other state and local governments have conducted their own studies regarding overturned criminal convictions in their own jurisdictions. It is the author's belief that at least part of these local government studies is due in part to bad publicity and upcoming election campaigns. We field more calls for information regarding eyewitness evidence as election years near. Governor George Ryan in the state of Illinois empaneled a Death Panel Review Committee (DPR).[8] The DPR committee recommended, in chapter 2 of their 2002 report, procedures very similar to those outlined in the Guide regarding eyewitness evidence, including the use of sequential and double blind procedures. That committee refers to the Guide as one of its sources for making some of its recommendations.

The state of Wisconsin formed the Avery Task Force after the court, in 2003, overturned the Manitowoc County rape conviction of Steven Avery, who spent eighteen years in the Department of Corrections for a crime he did not commit; his conviction was based largely on eyewitness testimony. At the conclusion of that body's work, the Wisconsin Attorney General, through the

---

[7] *State v. Larry R. Henderson*, New Jersey 2011

[8] Available at www.idoc.state.il.us/ccp/index.html

Wisconsin Department of Justice, Bureau of Training and Standards for Criminal Justice, issued a "Model Policy and Procedure for Eyewitness Identification"[9] in 2005. The policies adopted by that manual are also strikingly similar to those originally published in the Guide. Also, in 2005, the state of Wisconsin, in cooperation with the state Bar Association, and the law schools of Marquette University and the University of Wisconsin, formed the Criminal Justice Study Commission as a forum to address the inadequacies of the criminal justice system.

Changes to procedures in eyewitness evidence have occurred in numerous jurisdictions, including, but in no way limited to; Vermont, Washington, D.C., Washington State, Georgia, Suffolk County and Boston, Massachusetts and locations throughout California.

The state of Illinois also mandated a field study of eyewitness procedures that was subsequently conducted by the Chicago, Evanston and Joliet police departments.[10] The results of that study have been called into question, by some in the research community.

The state of Georgia established a subcommittee to examine the overturned convictions within their state during 2007. We testified before that subcommittee on October 1, 2007, and made suggestions that law enforcement personnel conducting identification procedures be trained before conducting any such procedures. We also suggested that each law enforcement agency develop its own written policy regarding eyewitness identification procedures. We agree that legislating exact procedures to be followed was unwarranted. The subcommittee subsequently recommended to the full general assembly the procedures we had suggested. The recommendations were forwarded to the general assembly under HB 997, the Witness Identification Accuracy

---

[9] Available at http://www.law.wisc.edu/fjr/clinicals/ip/ag_model_policy.pdf

[10] Available at www.chicagopolice.org/IL%20Pilot%20on%20Eyewitness%20ID.pdf

16

Enhancement Act.[11] While that bill was not codified, the Georgia POST commission did accept their suggestions and subsequently developed training that is strikingly similar to the Guide.

In 2009, the Supreme Judicial Council of Massachusetts formally accepted the procedures presented in the Guide."[12] That court failed to take a position on presentation method (sequential versus simultaneous). Note that this development came years after the Northampton, Massachusetts Police Department adopted a written policy that mandated sequential, double blind identification procedures as well as the use of formal instructions. (This was accomplished under the direction of author Captain Kenneth Patenaude.) That department became the first municipal law enforcement agency to voluntarily mandate these policy changes.

In early 2010, the New York State Justice Task Force began studying overturned convictions in that state. One of their main concerns was eyewitness evidence. Captain Patenaude gave a presentation to this task force on April 16, 2010.

During July of 2010, the U.S. House of Representatives passed a bill to create a National Criminal Justice Panel. This panel may examine the causes of wrongful convictions.[13]

The state legislature of Rhode Island in 2010 passed a measure creating an eight-member panel to identify procedures to prevent mistaken eyewitness identification. That panel, which met for the first time during August of 2010, submitted a final recommendation for policies, procedures and training to the Governor, State Supreme Court and the legislature in January 11, 2011. All law enforcement agencies within Rhode Island were to have written eyewitness evidence policies in place by June 11, 2011. Captain Patenaude gave a presentation to this body.

The state of Florida convened a twenty-three-member Florida Innocence Commission that met for its first meeting in September

[11] legis.state.ga.us/legis/2007_08/fulltext/hb997.htm

[12] See *Comm. v Silva-Santiago*, 453 Mass. 782

[13] From innocence project website, innocenceproject.org reviewed 8/25/10.

of 2010. This commission is studying the eleven Florida exonerations based mainly on faulty eyewitness evidence. A report from that body is due in June 2012.[14] It is of interest to note that this commission did not have any "front line" law enforcement officers among its members.

Finally, we wonder why commission after commission, in state after state, are formed throughout the country to review the same problem of overturned criminal convictions due to eyewitness error over and over. Is every commission trying to reinvent the wheel? As observed back when the United States Department of Justice formed the Technical Working Group for Eyewitness Evidence in 1998, the problems are no different jurisdiction to jurisdiction. Indeed, further research and continued overturned convictions reveal that the major common factor in all the cases is eyewitness errors.

Most of the eyewitness errors are "human" mistakes, but again research and analysis of the overturned cases has shown law enforcement procedure to be a large part of the problem. Why, we wonder doesn't the law enforcement community take the lead and enact the changes necessary?

An amazing story of one woman's misidentification that led to an overturned conviction of Ronald Cotton is illustrated in the 2009 book titled, *Picking Cotton.* The book is the cooperative effort of the victim, Jennifer Thompson-Canino and the convicted suspect, Ronald Cotton, who spent more than eleven years in the North Carolina prison system for crimes he did not commit.[15]

Also, on the mass media front, a full length movie *Conviction* was released for national audiences in theaters on October 15, 2010. That movie, starring Hilary Swank, retold the story of Betty Anne Waters who studied for years to become an attorney to defend her brother Kenny Waters. She believed him to be wrongfully convicted based in part on eyewitness evidence, and

---

[14] St. Petersburg Times, Tampa Bay & Florida news article 9/11/10

[15] Available St. Martin's Press

after extensive and determined resolve gained her brothers freedom and exoneration of all charges.

Even with all of this attention focused on the eyewitness identification issue; it is still common for us to hear many comments from persons who are still unfamiliar with the problems or the issues with the overturned convictions.

Why is this book necessary? That's the question most asked of us as we travel lecturing around the country. There is an ideology of our brethren who say to us, such things as; "we're better than that now, we've progressed, we are more educated, we don't need changes."

We acknowledge that law enforcement training has improved tremendously and forensic evidence has and continues to advance and mature. We do, however, point out that DNA evidence is found in only a very small percentage of cases. The DNA evidence is found in the most heinous crimes investigated by law enforcement, i.e., homicides and sex crimes. We believe that these are the types of cases where evidence collection is stressed. What happens to the majority of cases involving robberies, auto thefts and burglaries as well as other crimes? With DNA to prove or disprove the charge against an arrested person, we still rely on eyewitness identification evidence. That should tell us why reforms are not only needed, but required.

We, who have combined over sixty years of police experience (mostly in the detective or investigative units of their respective police departments), believe changes must be made in how law enforcement protects its crime scenes. They must be diligent in their efforts to look at and collect all possible evidence at every crime scene with the thought that technology is ever changing and their efforts may one day solve that crime. Police departments must have the courage to make the changes they see fit to correct any areas that may prevent innocent people from going to prison and that may assist in the arrest and conviction of the actual perpetrators. We ask you to review this work and make that decision for yourself.

We strongly believe that it is time to revise the Department of Justice publication to eliminate the simultaneous procedure and include the double blind administration process.

In the chapters that follow, we have relied heavily on their successful training programs they have given around the United States. As such, we will discuss the following topics:

How and why was the *Department of Justice Eyewitness Evidence Guide* developed? There will be a brief discussion of how your authors have found, through researchers' findings, human memory can be fallible. After all, an identification of a suspect is based on a memory of the incident. We also will discuss the techniques used in a cognitive interview. This process is meant to obtain a greater amount of accurate information from a cooperative witness or victim. Next, we cover identification procedures, such as; show-ups, lineups both photographic and digital image and live, how to pick fillers for these procedures along with composite drawings and pre-identification procedural instructions.

We also will review simultaneous versus sequential (one at a time) identification procedures, how to incorporate the double blind identification procedure (where neither the victim/witness nor the officer conducting the identification procedure know where the suspects image is in the identification procedure), witness bolstering and the duty to accurately report the events and comments of the procedure.

Finally, we want to state that the vast numbers of eyewitness identifications are obtained by dedicated law enforcement officials. The great majority of the thousands and thousands of eyewitness identifications are correct. We maintain however, that any small procedural change that can save an innocent person from going to prison for a crime they didn't commit is worth the effort.

Chapter 1
Reasons for Change

As it relates to eyewitness identification, social science researchers and academia have proven that the problem is clear and convincing, human memory is fallible. Throughout this book we will share with you the knowledge gained from several researchers and their findings combined with our expansive police experiences to help you understand the errors that could, and most likely, will occur during an eyewitness identification.

"Many Eyewitnesses Identify Wrong Person," is one of the many newspaper headlines that have appeared in recent years. This problem was noted by the United State Supreme Court more than forty years ago.[16] The problem was again highlighted, to a larger criminal justice audience, in June 1996 with the U.S. Department of Justice publication *Convicted by Juries, Exonerated by Science.*[17] That document reported, in great detail, the first twenty-eight overturned convictions with the use of actual physical evidence, Deoxyribonucleic acid (DNA). After years of hearings throughout state and federal courts, DNA evidence had become an accepted piece of physical evidence. Even a quick review of *Convicted by Juries, Exonerated by Science* showed that the vast majority (approaching 78%) of the original convictions were based largely on eyewitness testimony.

To date there are almost two hundred seventy-five overturned

---

[16] See *United States v Wade* 388 U.S. 218 (1967)

[17] Available at www.ncjrs.gov Search under NCJ 161258

convictions. This represents a minuscule percentage of all arrested persons identified by an eyewitness identification procedure each year. Considering those numbers alone, it would seem that law enforcement is doing a tremendous job. However, some in law enforcement saw that report as the tip of the iceberg or worried further that eyewitness identification evidence was really a house of cards destined to fall in on itself. If these exonerations are coming from only the homicide and sexual assault cases where the DNA evidence is most commonly collected, you must ask yourself how many innocent people are serving time as a result of being misidentified at a felony crime scene where DNA evidence is either not available or was not processed?

Further review of the data collected in those original twenty-eight overturned cases shows that some of the corroboration of the eyewitness evidence was as weak as having no alibi or based on questionable science that has since been discredited or no longer used because it is unreliable.

Police detectives are trained to corroborate every piece of evidence obtained during an investigation. We train the students to use the triangle form of investigation where each point of the triangle is connected with the next. The best cases include the three points of the triangle or elements of evidence, i.e.; physical, eyewitness and a confession. Each of those points or elements should corroborate the other. The best example of this type of investigation is detailed in the book by Truman Capote, *In Cold Blood* which details the November 1959 murders of the Clutter family in Holcomb, Kansas. The subsequent investigation, arrests and convictions caused by the Kansas Bureau of Investigation (KBI), is in our opinion, an example of the type of criminal investigation standard that should be practiced by every law enforcement agency worldwide.

Put another way, as David Simon stated as rule #2 of his Ten Rules of Homicide Investigation in his best-selling novel and subsequent television program, *Homicide, Life on the Street*, three things solve crimes; physical evidence, witnesses and confessions.[18] While most investigations do not obtain all three of the desired pieces of evidence, it is still the standard sought.

Eyewitness Identification

Physical Evidence   Confession

Another element of that training is a working knowledge of basic forensic evidence and its value. We are continually surprised to learn firsthand that a large portion of the students, both police and prosecutors, are unfamiliar with the value of trace or blood evidence collected at crime scenes. Microscopic hair analysis is really good for elimination purposes and ABO blood typing might be able eliminate only 10% of the population in some cases. These types of evidence are still examples of good science, but must also be considered in its proper perspective. If the evidence's value is overvalued or overstated to a jury, a wrongful conviction could easily occur.

Remember also that police procedures regarding witnesses and identifications have been unchanged over the last century. After all, in criminal justice circles the phrases we have heard from the class participants have ranged from, "We've never done it like that, we do it this way," "and 'we're getting convictions now, why should we change?'

A small percentage of the overturned convictions also included

---

[18] From: *Homicide, a Year on the Killing Streets*, 1991 by David Simon, Houghton Mifflin Company

a confession alleged to have been given by the defendant. We ask you to consider how and under what circumstances does a person who is found factually innocent with indisputable physical evidence, confesses to a crime he did not commit.

Adding to the list of problems, we often hear during training classes comments and rumblings such as, "Well if the guy didn't do that crime, he committed another crime that we didn't him catch for." Although this may be true, we do not believe that this is how our system should work nor should we condone such a thought process. Surprisingly, these comments come from both law enforcement officers and prosecutors. We feel that comments like this are based on frustration with the entire criminal justice system, rather than an actual comment about the wrongful conviction. The average person within the criminal justice system feels helpless to correct the system's shortcomings.

In contrast to this thought process is a case that occurred in Northampton where a registered sex offender was accused of a sexual assault and identified by the victim as he rode his bicycle through the police parking lot. This individual was arrested and processed. The investigators continued their investigation over the next several days while the identified perpetrator sat in jail. What the investigators learned was that the victim had lied about the sequence of events and eventually admitted it was a false claim. Although the registered sex offender had committed other crimes he did not commit this particular crime. What we stress to all of our students is that you must work just as hard to exonerate the innocent as you do to convict the guilty.

In response, we counter with the fact that one of the reasons that the subject may have been under suspicion for the crime is his prior record, or maybe because he is the local "bad guy."[19] We will admit that the vast majority of overturned convictions are persons with arrest records, but some of the defendants have very minor

---

[19] It is understandable that some law enforcement officers would feel this is the correct way to solve crimes. It is relayed to them from their first days in the police academy that a very percentage of persons are responsible for a large part of the overall crimes.

records from years ago and some even have no prior criminal record. Besides, isn't it our responsibility to find the person responsible? What good does it do to leave the real perpetrator walking around to commit other crimes?

During the past dozen years we have conducted our own informal survey of the thousands of class and seminar law enforcement officers regarding what, if any, formal training they have received or written policy they follow regarding eyewitness identification. The vast majority of the officers learned the procedures when a fellow officer, with some experience, instructs the younger officer or has the younger officer observe an identification procedure that is being conducted. We offer the possibility that the young officers may not have learned or understood all the intricacies there are to know about the eyewitness identification process. What if that officer learned the wrong way or has not been responsible for an identification procedure for some time?[20]

Compounding that particular circumstance we find that most law enforcement agencies do not have a written contemporary policy regarding eyewitness identification evidence.[21]

An informal question and answer session at each training shows that it appears even in those agencies with a written policy concerning eyewitness identifications, the department members failed to have any working knowledge of the policy. Indeed, one detective from a Missouri police department even mistakenly thought that a written identification instruction form constituted a formal written policy.

Regarding criminal court cases, it appears that it is almost impossible for the prosecution to lose a defense motion to suppress

---

[20] Indeed at each training session, we routinely ask the officers attending how many have had any formal eyewitness evidence training? It is very rare to see even one hand raised in response.

[21] Studies from Georgia and Texas reveal that from departments responding to a survey, only 13% have written policies. A more recent study from Rhode Island revealed that only 24% reported they have a written policy. This data is from 41 of 42 requested Rhode Island agencies.

an identification. To the police officers and prosecutors reading this, we ask you to try to recall the last time one of their identifications was suppressed, or even the last time they heard of an identification being suppressed?

Connecticut criminal defense Attorney, Lisa J. Steele, sums it up very nicely when she reports that Courts, for the most part, will not suppress identifications obtained under the traditional non-blind identification procedures, which are acceptable under the standards suggested by the U.S. Supreme Court in *Manson v. Braithwaite*, 432 U.S. (1977). Under *Manson*, if a court concludes that an identification procedure (show-up, lineup or array) was needlessly suggestive (the circumstances could have unnecessarily influenced the witness to identify the police suspect as the culprit), the trial court then considers the reliability of the identification. The reliability of an identification procedure is considered under various factors, such as the opportunity of the witness to view the criminal at the time of the crime, the witness's degree of attention, the accuracy of (his) prior description of the criminal, the level of certainty demonstrated at the confrontation, and the time between the crime and confrontation. Against these factors is to be weighed the corrupting effect of the suggestive identification itself. If the procedure is not deemed unnecessarily suggestive, the trial court never reaches the reliability analysis.[22]

Sgt. Carroll agreed to testify for the Public Defender's Office on a defense motion to suppress an alleged identification in a Los Angeles County criminal courtroom.[23] After reviewing the police reports regarding the alleged photo identification of a suspect during 2007 he provided sworn testimony that there was no identification by the witness. The reports prepared by the police and a transcript of a recording during the identification procedure showed that the officer conducting the procedure was the assigned case officer, he knew who the suspect was and specifically asked

[22] Adapting to new *Eyewitness Identification Procedures*, page 86, Thomson Reuters/Aspatore , 2010

[23] *California v. Gerardo* Cabrera BA 286262

the witness if the suspect was the person the witness had observed. When the witness stated his objections to this person, due to a visible tattoo on the suspect's neck the officer helped alleviate the witness' doubt by stating that the witness may have failed to remember the tattoo because the offender may have been wearing an outer garment with a collar during the crime. The judge declined to suppress the alleged identification on the basis that the identification was the only evidence that the prosecution had remaining.

In the rare case where a trial court excludes a pretrial identification procedure, an in court identification of the suspect (defendant) by a victim or witness is still permissible. It seems illogical that a witness or victim would ever have a difficult time recognizing the perpetrator in the jail clothing with the deputy sheriff sitting behind him. If the defendant is in a suit, how difficult is it to point to the person sitting next to the defense attorney? There are certain circumstances that the prosecutor may overcome the obvious suggestiveness of this identification. Among them (again) is the opportunity of the witness to view the criminal at the time of the incident, the witness's degree of detail, the accuracy of (his) prior description of the criminal, and the level of certainty (see our later chapter on certainty statements) demonstrated in court. When those factors are considered, depending on the answers, the in court identification of the defendant may be allowed.

Even a cursory review of the cases that have been overturned by the appellate courts shows that the greatest majority of the cases had faulty identification of witnesses in common. Depending on when you review those cases, between 75% and 82% of those cases depended in great part on an eyewitness identification. Add to this a study that indicated there is no stronger or compelling evidence presented in court than a victim or witness pointing in open court to the defendant and uttering words similar to, "That's the guy that shot me!"

One study that interviewed jury members after their service

concluded that jurors believe witnesses more than fingerprints!

Another issue facing us is that of human memory as it pertains to eyewitness identification, the major component of eyewitness evidence is misunderstood. We will review some of the points on human memory in another chapter.

The last, and perhaps most perplexing of all, is that when the criminal justice system convicts a truly innocent person, there is a tremendous burden placed on the defendant to successfully overturn the conviction. The biggest obstacle rests with the way our federal and local state constitutions are interpreted. The main right of a person post conviction is not "I'm innocent" but instead "you violated my rights.[24]

Actual innocence is a very difficult position to prove and indeed, the system now believes that person to be guilty. Prior to any conviction in court, the defendant is presumed innocent, but after a trial and upon a guilty verdict, the burden shifts from the prosecution to the defense. In normal cases (where the defendant is really guilty) this seems fair. However, if there is a mistake and an innocent person is convicted, that fact is very difficult to prove.

---

[24] *Herrera v Collins* where the US Supreme Court ruled that there is not a constitutional claim and is not a concern of the federal courts (1993)

Chapter 2
The DOJ Guidelines and
the Technical Working Group

Confronted with the conclusions reached with the publication of *Convicted by Juries, Exonerated by Science* then Attorney General Janet Reno tasked the National Institute of Justice, the Department of Justice's research arm, with identifying some way to change or alter the landscape of overturned convictions.

The U.S. Department of Justice has used the Technical Working Group (TWG) formula for some time over many disciplines in criminal justice.[25] The TWGs bring together subject matter experts for discussion and presentation of problems and solutions to a vast array of criminal justice issues. Several ground breaking Guides have been published and made available to all interested persons on the internet by way of the National Criminal Justice Research Service website.[26]

Once the subject matter experts have been identified, a meeting is arranged in a convenient location. The panel of experts that is drawn from every corner of the United States and is intended to bring together individuals from various occupations related to the criminal justice system and points of view. Those attending this introductory meeting get acquainted and discuss the identified

---

[25] Technical Working Groups (TWGs) exist for the future of DNA evidence, crimes scenes, fingerprints, digital evidence, arson and death investigations among many others. All have published guides relating to their specialties.

[26] www.ncjrs.gov

issue or problem. In the case of the Technical Working Group for Eyewitness Evidence (TWGEYEE), thirty-four persons were identified and selected to work with the TWG for the entire time necessary to bring forward a product. Our TWG of 34 committed professionals included seventeen police officers from throughout the country including large city, rural, local, county and state police personnel. The group included six prosecutors from large offices and small, five defense attorneys, including public defenders both local and federal, and six prominent eyewitness and human memory researchers.

The TWG for Eyewitness Evidence started its work during May 1998 and continued through October 1999. We met in different cities to minimize, where possible, the travel hardships and time constraints for the members. To say that working in a group of such diverse experiences, personalities and points of view was an extraordinary experience is an understatement.

Even before the meeting began, the stereo type associated with the various professions in the room was immediately evident. In one corner were the prosecutors, in the corner farthest away from them the defense attorneys were huddled together. The researchers were clumped together talking by the coffee pot and the police members mingled with every group.

One of the first lessons learned about this particular group dynamic was that each entity had its' own perspective. The prosecution wants to win their case and it *seems*, at times, that the win, at any cost, is their only goal. The defense is worried about winning also, (obtaining a not guilty verdict), and is truly worried about the rights of the defendant (their client). The researchers worry about the mistakenly identified defendant. There seems to be no concern on their part at all about a defendant unless she or he was mistakenly identified. The researchers were fond of saying that if the actual offender (perpetrator) is in the identification procedure, it doesn't matter what type of identification procedure (simultaneous or sequential) is used. The police are usually interested in prosecuting the real (actual) offender. This system we call criminal justice has become an adversarial one where the primary goal is to win. The system's focus must always be to strive for justice. Our view has always been and always will be that you must work just as hard to exonerate as you do to convict.

Another feeling that we have is that if the prosecution does not like the police theory of the case, the prosecutor seems to exert their authority about how to continue. This seems to go against reason as it is the police who thoroughly investigated the case long before the prosecution received their case. The reverse appears to be true with the defense attorneys. If the defense doesn't like what the police say about a case or procedure, they will, at least listen to the police officers position and often change their perspective.

It is generally known that once judicial proceedings have commenced[27] the suspect is entitled to have a lawyer present during any identification procedure. However, if an attorney arrives to view the ID procedure, that lawyer can only, at best, be an observer. She or he cannot make any comments, talk to the witnesses or get involved with the procedure in any way. Should the lawyer for the defense subsequently file a motion to suppress the ID, the lawyer can then be called by the prosecution as their witness and in essence become a state's witness.

Judges when confronted with a pretrial suppression motion from a defense attorney have been known to ask the attorney in open court why she or he failed to protest or make their objections known at the time of the ID procedure. The more experienced detectives, aware of this, will ask a defendant's lawyer to assist them in preparing the identification procedure by obtaining suggestions about fillers and where their client would like to be during the lineup.

Once this is explained to defense lawyers, most will refrain from attending lineup procedures.

The TWG set the following goals for its mission:

1-Increase the amount of information elicited from witnesses.

---

[27] Arrest warrant or indictment obtained

2-Heighten the validity/accuracy of the eyewitness obtained.

3-Improve the (criminal justice) systems ability to evaluate eyewitness evidence.

With our goals firmly set, the group got down to work over many weeks and months. Sometimes the discussions would turn loud. Due to the differing positions of the various participants it seemed at times, almost impossible to agree. After all, who in their right mind, would expect prosecutors, defense attorneys and police officers to agree on ANYTHING. Now, add to that mix of differing opinions, the academic field with research professors stressing their point of view on a subject that they had studied for many years, but who have no practical legal or street experience.

The TWG was fortunate to have Lisa Kaas as the NIJ's facilitator. Lisa had this extraordinary ability to listen to all the different raised voices and opinions and was able to translate those sounds into coherent words and sentences. We are reasonably certain that without Lisa's talent, the eyewitness guide never would have made it to final publication. The final Guide is therefore, a consensus document.

We would like to point out however, that each disagreement was strictly from a professional point of view or reference. Somehow, each evening we seemed to continue discussing the points of the project over dinner and cocktails. A great number of long-lasting friendships were developed over the length of the project. Many of the members are in regular contact with each other and maintain close professional relationships.

The subsequent Eyewitness Evidence Guide was to be based on the following principles:

1-Research has shown that memory can be (is) fragile.

2-The amount and accuracy of the information obtained from eyewitnesses depends in part on the method of questioning.

3-Application of scientific principles and current good (best) practice allows us to obtain the best eyewitness evidence possible.

The resulting Guide has been used as a model for many law enforcement agencies. According to Lt. Jonathyn W. Priest,

Commander of the Denver, Colorado Police Department's Crimes Against Persons-Homicide-Major Crimes Section the significance of this report is that many law enforcement agencies adopted the language from the guide in creating their identification protocols and procedures.[28] Not a bad endorsement in our minds.

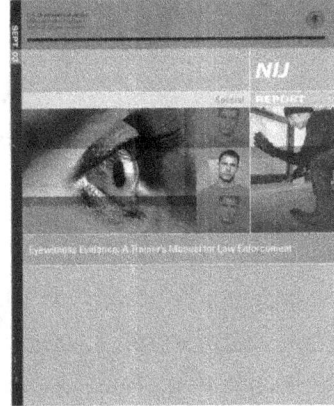

These Department of Justice publications may be obtained from the following website:

http://www.ncjrs.gov/pdffiles1/nij/178240.pdf &

http://www.ncjrs.gov/nij/eyewitness/188678.pdf

---

[28] Adapting to new Eyewitness Identification Procedures, page 44, Thomson Reuters/Aspatore , 2010

Chapter 3
Human Memory

The original publication was complete with a chapter that went into some detail concerning human memory. The researchers convinced most of the TWG members that a basic understanding of how memory works was essential to understanding the problem with misidentifications and the subsequent wrongful convictions.

Post publication and after a new administration was entrenched, the National District Attorney's Association expressed its concern that research on human memory was really more art than science. They pressured the new administration at the Justice Department to remove any mention of human memory in subsequent editions of the Guide.

We received quite a few telephone calls from criminal justice professionals, including judges, who were at a loss to understand the purpose of the guide without the human memory references. The callers quickly understood the guide's intent when they received the memory explanation.

It seems almost humorous now, as we write this sequel to the Guide, because prosecutors have lately been among the most vocal leaders in advocating for the policy changes we recommended when the guide was originally published.

As we have stated, we are not academics or scientific researchers. We are merely law enforcement officers with some extensive background and experience in police investigative technique. Part of that experience is how to conduct criminal investigations and attempting to understand the dynamics of the witnesses and victims.

In that limited capacity, we will endeavor to explain the processes involved regarding human memory and its effect on remembering the offender in a crime. We hope to dispel the many misconceptions about human memory that many of us harbor.

One of the many useful suggestions regarding human memory obtained from the researchers within the TWG is the trace evidence perspective suggested by Professor Gary Wells, Ph. D of Iowa State University. The idea is to think of eyewitness evidence as a form of trace evidence; something that the suspect left at the scene of the crime. Unlike physical evidence, this trace cannot be observed or placed in an evidence container. This trace is in the victim's or witness's mind and it may well lead to the identity of the offender. This evidence is delicate and can easily be compromised, destroyed or damaged if mishandled. Evidence may be cross contaminated and will decay over time. Studies indicate that human memory will decline fairly rapidly in which case it is important that the first responders and investigators understand the necessity of obtaining this fragile evidence as soon as possible.

% Level of Memory

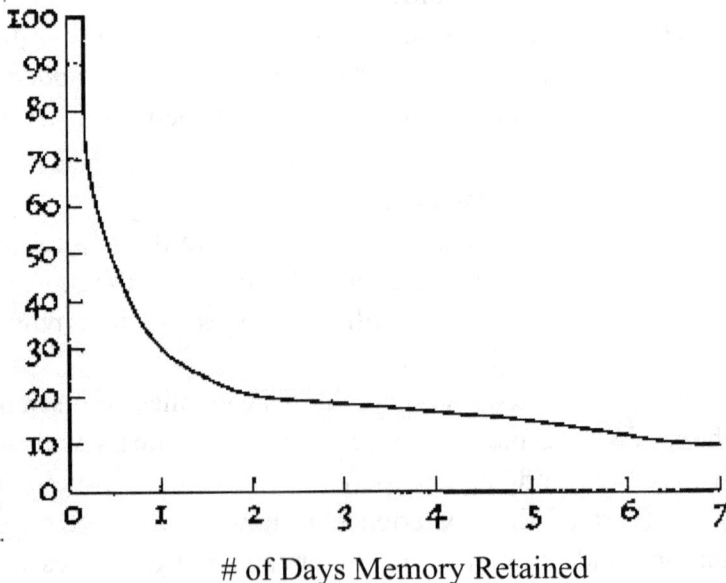

# of Days Memory Retained

In 1885, German philosopher, Hermann Ebbinghaus tested memory retention ability using himself as the test subject and found that he remembered less than 40% after only nine hours had passed but the rate of forgetting leveled off over a period of time.

We have learned that there are two types of memory, long term and short term. Long term memory is nearly unlimited. Some things are memorized once and never forgotten. Take for example a giraffe or your birth date.

While we have found that this is a correct concept, those who interview suspects and witnesses have also found that while everyone knows what a giraffe looks like, everyone remembers the giraffe a little differently. Some people forget about the pompom type tail, or the giraffe has both horns and ears. Some will elongate the body or the animal's legs. So while everyone knows what a giraffe is there are differences in the way different persons remember or recall the animal.

Also be aware of the idea of garbage in, garbage out. Take, for example, a person whose parents altered their birth date to get them enrolled in school one year early. It is conceivable that person has incorrect information to make a true statement.

Short term memory, is as the title suggests, i.e., short. Think of looking up a phone number to call for a pizza. You'll probably remember the number just long enough to make the call. (if you're like us, sometimes you'll forget the number before you can complete the call). After you dial the telephone number, you forget the number.

Human memory process takes three distinct processes:

Acquisition: When an event is perceived.

Retention: Time between acquisition and information recall.

Retrieval: Time when acquired information is recalled.

The main misconception to remember is that memory is NOT like a video/digital camera. You cannot simply hit the rewind button on the VCR and play back exactly how the event transpired. We also learned that human memory works differently for each individual. We process and recall events based upon our attention to various details and individual perceptions. Your memory of an event can decay rather quickly and because of this fact police officers must attempt to retrieve as much information from the witnesses as soon as possible.

Another misconception about memory is that everyone seeing the same thing will have the same recollection regarding that activity. We have learned that perception is different among different people. During our classes we display an image which includes an older woman and a young woman. While results differ, we have never taught a class about memory where everyone saw both women without being shown which is which. When polling our audience the majority either sees the older woman or the younger woman, but few can see both women.

Keep in mind also that expectation affects the way you process information observed.

These classes are shown a series of descending circles, and to date, no student has correctly identified the object. The object is immediately perceived as a spiral. We are also known to have an unsuspecting class member repeat ten times, very fast, the words displayed on the screen, usually a dog identified as Spot and a stop sign, identified as stop. (Spot-stop, Spot-stop, Spot-stop, etc.) Just before the tenth repetition we continue to the next slide. This slide displays a red stop light and the following question, what do you do at a green light? In response to that question, something approaching 75% reply STOP. When asked again, they repeat STOP. We have on occasion had students answer stop up to four times before realizing their mistake.

The witness' expectation of what occurred may cloud their statement of what actually occurred. Perceptions and expectations are not objective but very subjective and criminal investigators must understand this is why when you have multiple witnesses involved in recounting an incident you will in most cases get several different accounts of the same event.

The next error we try to expose regarding human memory tells us that not everything that is attended to (observed) is remembered.

This short exercise we use explains some of the main problems in eyewitness evidence. The entire afternoon session of eyewitness evidence training programs can be based on this simple exercise.

We display a group of pennies and ask the class to identify the position of the real penny. Sometimes we post a target absent display, i.e., a slide without a real penny and sometimes the slide contains the real penny. Our experience reveals that less than 15% of the students pick the real penny when it is displayed and less than 10% state that the real penny is not present when it is not among those displayed. We explain to the majority of the class that selected a penny from that slide that in real life had just sent an innocent penny to prison because the real penny is NOT present on that slide. This leads to a dual injustice when an innocent person goes to prison and the guilty person is free to commit more crimes.

Many of the students (usually more than 40%) pick the example of a penny that shows items from the front and back of a real penny. Consider also, that there are usually at least a few persons present who had coin collections as teenagers.

A few students comment, after viewing the target absent slide, that you didn't warn us that the real penny might not be present.

The class is then reminded that pre-identification procedural instructions will be discussed later but that their observation is valid and to remember how important that instruction might be during criminal cases.

Another slide is shown with two quarters, two dimes and two nickels, one correct and one false. The participants are normally divided 50% to 50% about which is the actual coin.

We continue by attempting to elicit the student's mechanics of how they came to their conclusions regarding the pennies. It takes some effort. Their methods are usually a process of elimination of those which couldn't be the correct one. Almost no one ever goes directly to their identified choice. That is, the participants first decided which penny could not be the correct one, eliminate those and then made a choice from those that were remaining. This is an example of a lesson for later in the program, identified as relative judgment.

Sergeant Carroll's favorite memory exercise involves a slide that covers all the numbers and letters on a telephone. First we ask the location of a certain letter. The correct answers are usually forthcoming, but you can readily observe students reaching for their cell phones or mimic touch dialing a telephone to remember. Some mistakenly remember the letters ABC on the number 1.

In the last exercise with the telephone we ask the class participants how many letters are on a telephone. After many strange looks we ask which two letters are missing? For those older students present, they KNOW that there are twenty-four letters on a telephone dial (key pad) and that the letters Q & Z are missing. Those students remember three letters to a number, numbers 2 through 9, total 24. Some then remember Q or Z as missing; most students only remember one of the missing letters. However, younger students (who use their telephones for texting) realize that all twenty-six letters are present on a telephone key pad. When shown a slide with a current phone, all now seem to remember.

Or Are They?

Another fact we impart is that memory is a constructive process. We ask the police officers present to remember their first wedding or any significant event and to think of this event for a moment. We then ask, can you see yourself at the event? A large portion of the class remembers seeing themselves at the event. Of course, that is impossible. They may have seen photos or remember a video, but it is obviously impossible to see yourself. How many people remember things that were impossible to view? It is a constructive process when you see yourself in this event.

There are two types of memory errors. These errors are referred to as errors of commission and errors of omission. Errors of omission occur when someone is unable to remember things that occurred. For example, when a police officer asks the witness to tell them what happened, some things may not be remembered at the time. The officer or an investigator must follow up with the witness because many times a witness will remember further details later. It is essential that an officer call the witness and follow up because the witness may not feel whatever detail they forgot to tell the officer originally is important. Errors of commission occur when facts are remembered are those details offered by the witness that are either not their memory but that of what someone else may have said or a detail that never occurred at all.

Memory error rates are influenced by two factors, things that are controllable and things that are not controllable. Those uncontrollable factors in criminal cases include time of day, lighting, the amount of time involved, a weapon focus (where victims see only a VERY BIG GUN), distance, cross racial (research suggests that people are better at identifying those of their own race) and stress level. An investigator cannot control these factors listed, however it is important that an investigator or police officer take note of all of these factors so when and if necessary, they can go back and recreate the circumstances, as much as reasonably possible, to observe from the witness vantage point what they could or could not see. You may be surprised at what you see or don't see!

The controllable factors include how the victim/witness is questioned, structure of the questions and pre-event instructions of the identification procedure. As a rule, we believe that if you control what you can and forget about what you can't control, you have done yourself a great favor.

Chapter 4
The Cognitive Interview

This chapter deals with questioning techniques when the person being interviewed is a cooperative witness or victim. It is designed to be used with persons who have important information and want to cooperate with law enforcement officials. The following recommendations are not meant to be used during the questioning or interview of a possible suspect.

The cognitive interview techniques have been in existence since the publication of the groundbreaking text by Drs. Ronald Fisher, Ph. D and R. Edward Geiselman, Ph. D in 1992.[29] We find that, while most investigators use some of the suggested practices (probably by trial and error), most law enforcement officers receive little or no interview training of the victim(s) or witness (es). Most of the formal interview training comes during the very early stages at the police academy when the officer is taught the 5 W's & how technique.[30] We feel that this may be adequate for the first responder or if you are preparing to write a short newspaper story. As every investigator/detective knows, in the world of investigative interviewing, the 5 W's and how leaves much to be desired. When conducting a follow up criminal investigation, the basis for the subsequent investigation and prosecution is based in large part on the quality of the preliminary (first responding

---

[29] Memory-Enhancing Techniques for Investigative Interviewing, The Cognitive Interview, Charles C. Thomas Publications

[30] Who, what, why, when and where

officer) investigator's interview of the victim and witnesses and the preparation of their police report.

As we have reported earlier, human memory is fragile and hence should be accessed and recorded as soon as possible. We suggest that the investigator treat victims and witnesses statements as a form of trace evidence. Remember that all trace evidence is very fragile and is subject to being lost or mishandled if not properly obtained and documented.

Due to the relatively inadequate interview training that law enforcement officers receive, the cognitive interview was developed. During tests with officers during clinical research and through actual cases, it has been determined that when using the techniques developed for the cognitive interview more accurate information is obtained without obtaining more false information.[31] The actual increase in correct information obtained from victims and witnesses was between 35% and 75%[32] when compared to usual police interview procedures.

The research conducted by Fisher & Geiselman was very informative. Some of the conclusions they came to were especially enlightening and they offer an in depth look into how police officers conduct interviews. For example, they discovered that the typical description obtained includes only about five descriptors, such as sex, age, race, hair or facial hair and height or build. Officers ask too many closed ended questions[33] and too few open ended questions.[34] They frequently interrupt the witness in the middle of a response. The typical police interview contains less than four open ended questions and when the witness answers, the officer interrupts within seven and one-half (7.5) seconds.

---

[31] Science Digest, Vol. XVI, pages 246-7

[32] RP Fisher & ML McCauley, *Informational Retrieval: Interviewing Witnesses,* Psychology & Policing,, 1995

[33] Limits the amount or scope of information a witness can provide, i.e.; was the car red?

[34] Allows for an unlimited response, i.e.; tell me in your words what happened?

Worst of all, in the author's mind, is the fact that the questions asked are usually in a predetermined, inflexible order. We refer to that method of questioning as the fill in the box mentality. We believe this occurs because the preliminary investigator is completing the police report asking questions that correspond to the boxes or position on the report as they are formatted by the computer software program being used by the particular department.

A person's mind does not remember events or descriptions in any set or predetermined order. Each person's memory operates in an individual and unique fashion. Therefore each individual remembers or recalls things and events differently. If the interviewee wants to describe the suspect's footwear first, then jacket, then height followed by hair length, and so on then that should be allowed. Interrupting the witness will only ensure that details will be forgotten or missed. For example, simply ask the witness to a crime, "Please describe the perpetrator."

Officers seem to forget that they were not present at the time of the offense, the victim or witness has the information, yet the officer dominates the interview and the victim or witness answers passively.[35] Interviewers should advise the victim/witness that they have the information needed and should tell the officer everything of the event as *they remember it.*

---

[35] R. Clifford and B.R. George *Making the Most of Witnesses*, Policing Magazine VIII, pages 185-198, 1992

The differences between the typical police interview and the cognitive interview are interesting to view side by side:[36]

Police Interview:	Cognitive Interview:
No (Little) Formal Training	Actual Techniques
Rapport not seen as important	Rapport seen as critical
Joe Friday Style (just the facts ma'am)	Open, non-authoritative
Witness Concentration not a high priority	Officer will not lead, but facilitates
No assistance offered to witness	Encourage concentration, convey needs
Police seen as manipulative	Assist witness to open retrieval pathways

The main components of the cognitive interview are human memory and communication skills. As we review the procedures of the cognitive interview techniques, take note that many of the procedures are very similar to a good interrogation. The cognitive interview consists of the following four principles; social dynamics, facilitation of the victim's thinking and memory, communication between the interviewer and the witness, and sequencing the interview.

Let us start at the end and explain the sequencing first. This is where the investigator plans an outline of how and where the interview should occur. First, no matter where the interview takes place, the officer should attempt to minimize the victim's anxiety and any distractions. If the interview occurs at a police facility, a cup of tea or coffee could be in order. Use of an interview room at this time will keep the victim out of the sight of other officers and others present.

---

[36] RP Fisher, E. Mello, ML McCauley *Are Jurors' Perception of Eyewitness Credibility Affected by the Cognitive Interview?* Psychology, Crime & Law V, pages 167-176,

Social Dynamics includes establishing and maintaining rapport between victim and officer, treating the victim or witness as an individual, encouraging the person to volunteer information and finally (the hardest for officers) is to be an active, attentive listener. You can establish and maintain a rapport with your victim similar to the early stage of an interrogation where you would find a common ground, for example, you may have attended the same school, are fans of the same sports team or served in the same military service. Asking about the injury that occurred during the crime might be your lead in. You will then explain to the victim that they were there when this happened, you weren't, so I need you to tell me everything that occurred. Remind the victim that a narrative from them is much more detailed than you asking questions, because you weren't there during the incident and you may not know exactly what to ask. (Remember just like in an interrogation it is better for a narrative response than a question and answer statement, i.e.; "Were you robbed?" Yes" "Were you on the street?" "Yes" "Was it at the corner of 7th and Main?" "Yes")

Remind the victim, prior to their statement to mentally recreate the circumstances. After their narrative rendition, ask specific questions to elicit details left out. Then you should review your notes and clarify any ambiguous information, i.e.; "My notes say _____, is that what you meant to say, or did I get that wrong?" Asking the witness about what they have reported ensures that the information has been understood and accurately recorded. Next, and we know that you have heard this many times before (but always seem to forget to ask it) ask the victim or witness "Is there anything else that I should have asked you"? (Note this is similar at the end of an interrogation when you ask the offender, is there anything that you wish to add or delete from this statement at this time?) You can now close the interview by thanking the person for their time, offering more coffee or tea and/ or a ride home. Also, offer your business card and remind them to call you when they remember more details (and they will, if they don't call you remember to call them).

The development of rapport between the witness and investigator will make the witness more comfortable during the interview process. Comfortable witnesses will generally provide more information. During the course of developing a rapport with the witness, the investigator can learn about the witness's communication style (e.g., how the witness describes everyday events compared with how the witness describes the incident).

A simple question, such as, "How are you doing," will not only contribute to rapport development, but it can alert the investigator to physical or mental conditions (e.g., intoxication, medication, shock) that could potentially impair the witness's ability to recall or report information effectively. Again, use open-ended questions. For each new topic of information being sought, the investigator should begin with open-ended questions and augment them with closed-ended questions, if necessary. For example, if, after having elicited all information from the witness about the perpetrator, the next topic of information is the getaway car, the investigator should begin this line of inquiry with open-ended questions about the car (e.g., what can you tell me about the vehicle).

Most of us, due to our nature and profession are used to being in control. In this context, however, it is much more productive to understand that you will gain more information by listening to the victim or witness narrative responses than if you attempt to control the direction by constantly interrupting and asking questions. In our classes, we compare listening to returning to the dating scene. Those that listen are referred to as kind, compassionate and interested, while those who dominate the conversation and who are constantly talking about themselves will soon become serial daters because they are unable to get a second date with the same person. A pause by the victim/witness may be the opportunity they need to attempt further recall and provide more details, its okay for a few seconds to pass as they try to remember.

Facilitation of the victim's memory and thinking includes ensuring that distractions are minimized during the interview. We are aware that most, if not all, of us were taught in a police academy a long time ago, that you interview at their house and you interrogate at your house. Broken down that statement refers to the commonly held belief that it's best to interview victims and witnesses where it is most comfortable for them and it is best to interrogate suspects at a law enforcement facility where the suspect is uncomfortable and at a disadvantage. Research has shown that you can elicit more information when you control the environment where the conversation takes place. This may only be possible for follow up interviews by investigators, but we believe even officers assigned to patrol duties can move the person interviewed out of the view of others or into a room in a hospital

Take for example you are assigned to interview the victim of a purse snatching. Assuming you are the preliminary investigating officer, you can probably use your patrol vehicle for the interview (turning off or down your radio). If however, you are the detective assigned to the follow up investigation, most of us would make an appointment with the victim to go to their house for the interview. Imagine, if you will, the following sequence of events. You arrive at the victim's house at the appointed hour. You observe that the victim's house is older, but is in good shape, the lawn is mowed with flowers in the garden. You knock on the door and wait for a response. You then ring the doorbell, mumbling under your breath. Suddenly, a Great Dane jumps up on the front door and starts barking (the dog is taller than you). Finally the victim comes to door and opens it. She greets you with the usual don't worry, he doesn't bite. After a moment, the victim locks up the dog (although he continues to bark). You are finally allowed in and suddenly the victim's cat appears at you feet and makes a figure eight motion around your ankles, leaving clumps of hair on your socks and trouser legs. You are then offered a seat on the couch (which is covered with cat hair). You finally clear a small portion on one of the cushions and sit down. Before you can ask the victim how she is, the telephone rings and the victim excuses herself. You note that the television is on rather loud and you can hear a baby crying upstairs. At this point you are thinking that this was a bad idea and you should have asked the victim to come to your office where you control the environment.

Using this method you can also overcome the notion commonly held by the defense bar that the only purpose of those empty rooms surrounding the squad room, is for interrogation or torture of their client. I have heard quite a few defense attorneys refer to them as dungeons. You can now respond when asked in court that those rooms are used to interview suspects, victims and witnesses. Remember also to identify these rooms as interview not as interrogation.

Now that you have controlled the environment, you attempt to have the victim mentally recreate the circumstances surrounding the incident. This can be accomplished in a number of ways. We usually ask the victim to think back to moments before the incident and begin to recall the events as they unfolded and "Remember that the offender said_____ to you." If the offender took the lord's name in vain, insert that in the blank. That might trigger a memory. In one case a victim was told by the offender that she was too old to have sex. That infuriated the victim and returned her memory to the moment of the crime. It's possible that even a smell could remind the victim of the incident and may trigger the best memories. In that event the interviewer might remind the victim of that fragrance or the fact that the offender smelled of cigarette smoke or alcohol.

During this part of the process, try to refrain from asking questions for more details. The witness should be encouraged to volunteer information without prompting. Because the witness, rather than the interviewer, possesses the relevant information, the witness should be mentally active during the interview and generate information, as opposed to being passive and waiting until the interviewer asks the appropriate question before answering. Encouraging the witness to actively generate information can be accomplished by stating expectations. This is important because witnesses may not know what to expect or may have incorrect expectations of their role in the interview. The interviewer should state explicitly that the witness is expected to volunteer information.   Interrupting the witness during his/her answer discourages the witness from playing an active role and disrupts his/her memory. Rather than interrupt, the interviewer should make a note and follow up later with any questions that arise during a witness's narration. However, if you feel that you must get a detail now, only ask the victim about what they are speaking of at that time. For example, if the victim is describing the weapon carried by the offender, don't ask about the offender's hair. It is better to remember your questions and get missing details after the victim has completed his/her statement.

Communication between the witness and interviewer consists of informing the interviewee of the interviewer's investigative needs.   What type of information and how much detail the investigator wants?   Second, you want to make the victim comfortable and encourage them to be at ease and communicate in a way that is easiest for them. By that we mean that some people talk with their hands as well as their voices, so gestures should be encouraged when appropriate. (A brief example we use in our classes is that of Sgt. Carroll's daughter. We inform the class that if she were handcuffed, she wouldn't be able to talk at all). Some victims are comfortable using or making drawings. In a recent case a victim related that she was a good artist and she could draw a sketch of the offender. The victim was left alone for a few minutes and when she was rejoined it was learned that she had produced a stick figure. While this may seem silly and unhelpful, that few minutes taken to draw that figure returned the victim to the time of the crime and rendered the following interview much more valuable. Last, but not least, it is very important for your victim or witness to understand that they should never guess. If there is something they don't know or remember it is all right;

guessing is not. (This may happen when a victim or witness wants to *really* help the officer or detective.)

When attempting to retrieve additional information from the witness, the following list of suggestions may be useful.

Change perspective: Ask to victim to pretend they were in a different part of the crime scene at the time of the offense. When describing a robbery, the victim may only recall and relate the actual offense. When asked to change their perspective, a victim should be encouraged to think more thoroughly about their experience. A useful example is a store clerk who has just been robbed at gunpoint. If asked to describe the offense and offender, the clerk is likely to describe only the gun and offender, with very little detail. If it is suggested that he pretend that he was the surveillance camera, the clerk may well remember when the suspect first entered the store, where he walked around, what the offender touched and may remember more details of the suspect. If you are going to use this change your perspective prompt stress that the victim must not guess about the details and must report only actual memories.

Use the alphabet to recall names: This technique may work in instances where there are multiple offenders and one called the other by name or in cases where the offender wore a shirt with his name or a logo. If the victim or witness is unable to recall the name, ask him or her to use the alphabet to help. Have them start at the letter "A" and try to recall or visualize names that start with each letter of the alphabet. In our experience, the interviewer can almost see the witness going through the alphabet in their mind.

Recall the event in a different order: Here is another way to shake the victim or witness to use more of their memory. After we have heard the witness account of the crime, we often ask our witness, from the time you called 9-1-1, tell me *backwards* what happened. After some thought, the witness will attempt to recount the incident as requested. If the interviewer is observant, s/he will observe the eyes of the witness looking up (and right for a right handed witness, opposite for a left handed witness). Those familiar with interrogation techniques will remember that a truthful right handed person looks up and right when telling the truth (accessing the memory part of the brain) and to the left when fabricating (accessing the fantasy portion of the brain). This is exactly opposite for a left handed person. This technique forces the witness to stop and really think about the events that occurred. We have obtained a large amount of additional information from witnesses when asking this question alone.

For the skeptical reader, try counting from one to one hundred, then count backward from one hundred to one. The reader will note that you will go much slower as you remember the numbers in a different sequence. Try also spelling you last name, then spell it backwards, it becomes much more deliberate as you must take your time to recount the appropriate order of the letters.

License Plates: There are a couple of tricks to help a witness remember a license plate (or tag) number. Good question to ask are "were the characters all numbers? Were they all letters? Was the plate a combination of letters and numbers"? The interviewer might also ask were the numbers high or low? Some years ago we were accustomed to asking about the color or design of the plate or tag to assist in determining the state of issue. These days many states produce license plates with different colors and backgrounds to sell as novelty or designer licenses for a revenue source. Indeed, the state of Florida has well over one hundred different license tags, some for colleges or sports teams or causes like saving the manatees.

Did the offender(s) remind you of anyone? In our experience, this is the single best question to assist the witness's memory and obtain more information about the offender for the investigator. If the witness informs the officer that, "Yes, he looked like my uncle Steve" the officer should continue with a simple "tell me how he resembles Uncle Steve. At this time the interviewer will get details that haven't been disclosed prior about the bad guy. It is not uncommon for the witness to respond with something like well for one thing they both have a similar scar over their right eye, or he is missing a finger on his left hand. These details will usually contain previously unreported facts. One series of cases some years back in Chicago involved the armed robberies of several small commercial establishments. The offender was usually described as a generic male about 30 years of age with short hair and glasses. An older detective re-interviewed the witnesses and asked each if the offender reminded them of anyone. Several victims then reported that the offender was an exact double for Mike Singletary, except smaller.[37] When queried further on this latest description the victims went on to describe the flat haircut, square jaw, square glasses, and intense stare, trademarks of Singletary who was a local professional football hero. This description was broadcast to officers in the area of the crimes and a suspect was located later that day. After further investigation the suspect was charged with over fifteen counts of armed robbery.

While discussing memory, we want to remind the reader that the dispatcher is an important player in the process. If the dispatcher uses closed ended questions rather than open ended questions, or offers information about the incident or asks leading questions, it can influence the way the witness recounts the events when interviewed in person by on officer. The dispatcher is, in effect, the first person on the scene of almost every event or crime.

The first responding law enforcement official has many responsibilities, including protecting the victim/witnesses memory. In addition to their normal duties of rendering first aid, apprehending the perpetrator, determining what crime, if any, occurred, protecting the scene, broadcasting an updated description of the offender s/he must verify the identity of witnesses, separate those witnesses so they cannot influence each other's memories and then canvass the area (search) for additional witnesses (GOYAKOOMD, i.e.: get off your ass knock on one more door) AND, if the offender is present or nearby, s/he must make an arrest. After those things have been accomplished, s/he must then

---

[37] At that time, Singletary was a famous linebacker for the Chicago Bears football team and local hero. He was later the head coach for the San Francisco Giants.

conduct an investigation and document what occurred and what was learned during that investigation in a completely detailed report. Information obtained from the witness can corroborate other evidence (e.g., physical evidence, accounts provided by other witnesses) in the investigation. Therefore, it is important that this information be accurately documented in writing. The preliminary investigation is critical as it forms a sound basis for the accurate collection of information and evidence during any subsequent follow-up investigation.

Post event contamination is when one witness shares their recall of the events with other witnesses prior to any police interview that may cause other witnesses memories to become contaminated with details not their own (e.g., the first witness mentions the suspect having a large nose and other witnesses then repeat this same detail to the police when interviewed, the question becomes, is this the actual memory of the other witnesses or the contamination by the first witness comment).

There was a case in Northampton, Massachusetts where a homicide was committed in the downtown area of the city on a very busy Friday afternoon. One teenager had stabbed another killing him in front of many eyewitnesses. The officers had done a fantastic job in gathering the witnesses and directing them to the lobby of the police department so that the investigators could interview them. Unfortunately, the lobby of the police department is approximately 20' long by 10' wide and there were ten to twelve witnesses waiting in the lobby. What occurred here is what we refer to as post event contamination where witnesses share information about the event they had just witnessed with others at the scene. In this case the group had a conversation about the obvious horrific scene they had just witnessed. It was difficult to determine from the witnesses what it was they witnessed versus what others had shared with them that became their memory.

We believe strongly that investigators must revisit witnesses after the first interview because witnesses will remember further details, albeit they may be minute in nature nonetheless those details may assist in the investigation.

The preliminary investigator(s) are additionally charged with informing the witnesses not to speak to other potential witnesses or the media. Media information may contaminate the witness's memory. Media requests for a story or offers of compensation may encourage a witness to fabricate information. Reporters may ask leading and closed questions that may alter memory.

An effort should also be made to have the witnesses contact either the officer or detectives when additional facts are recalled.[38]

We would like to dispel a myth at this point. It is important to be aware that research has proven that just because a witness is wrong about one fact concerning the incident or description that does *not* predict the accuracy of the additional information.

---

[38] Studies reveal that most victims/witnesses recall more details but are reluctant to contact police feeling that their information is trivial.

Chapter 5
Digital Image (Photograph)
Collection and Display

Back in 1999, when the original eyewitness evidence guide was drafted, mug books still existed and were a common way to display photographs (images) of suspects. At that time we wrote: *Mug books (i.e., collections of photos of previously arrested persons) may be used in cases in which a suspect has not yet been determined and other reliable sources have been exhausted. This technique may provide investigative leads, but results should be evaluated with caution.*

Non-suggestive composition of a mug book may enable the witness to provide a lead in a case in which no suspect has been determined and other reliable sources have been exhausted. We presented the reader with guidelines for storing and displaying the photographs.

With the emergence of digital imaging technology and storage over the last decade (or so) the procedures for obtaining, storing and displaying images of criminal suspects has changed significantly. As mentioned before there is an entire generation of police officers who have no idea what a mug book is.

Some of those procedures regarding the showing of suspect's images remain the same. First it is essential that the official conducting any type of identification procedure with human images make it clear to the viewer that the images that are being shown are a "collection of photographs or images." These images should not be referred to as "gang members" or "known robbers."

It is important to note here that prior to digital imaging technology being integrated into law enforcement, a common practice regarding booking or arrest photographs was to wait until a suspect's fingerprints had "cleared" and the arrestee had been positively identified. This was a good policy for a number of reasons. If the photographs of arrestees were filed by FBI number or SID (state identification number) or IR (identification record) number it didn't matter then, what name the subject was arrested under. His fingerprints positively identified him and the photograph was supplemental. For those law enforcement agencies with policies that required taking an arrest photo only every three or five years, this saved quite a few dollars. However, with the advances in digital imaging technology, some departments now take an image of the same individual at almost every booking process. Some physical characteristics may change, such as; length of hair, hair color, additional or reduced amounts facial hair, additional tattoos, scars or other markings or changes. Without a review function to ensure that the suspect's FBI, SID or IR is inserted on the image, the image is now filed under arrest number or CB (central booking) number. The problem for follow-up investigators, when attempting to obtain images of suspects or fillers for identification procedures, is the fact that there may be numerous images of the same person in the digital file with many aliases. This could create a serious problem in court if this is not anticipated by the lineup administrator.

Second there must be positive identifying information for each image or picture shown. While this procedure seems obvious to detectives and those who normally conduct follow-up investigations, newer officers and those officers not used to being held accountable may not be fully aware of the importance of having proper identification for each photograph or digital image. What we are saying here is that it is not proper procedure to use a confiscated gang photo where the people displayed in the image are flashing gang signs, and pointing guns.

Third, official department booking images are the best for use in photo array procedures. Backgrounds on the photographs

57

should be similar, when possible, as they would be when using booking images. However, we recommend against using photos or images with height markings. This severely limits your choice of filler photos as each filler would necessarily be about the same height (within an inch or so). The other possibility here is that all the backgrounds should be different or the same. Altering the backgrounds of non-suspect/filler pictures might be one possibility, or blurring the backgrounds would also be allowable. The idea here, as explained in court decisions, is that no photo should *unduly* standout.[39] Another problem when assembling photos for an identification procedure is the clothing worn by those depicted in the photos. Booking photos at county jails tend to be taken in jail uniforms. This satisfies the problem of someone unduly standing out, but we feel it is difficult to pick out the real suspect if the depicted persons look like clones. We think it is better to everyone displayed in a different color shirt. We also understand that this will probably lead the defense bar toward questions where the attorney will ask "isn't it true detective, that my client is the only person depicted in the lineup with a white shirt?" or motions to suppress the out of court identification which state the same fact. The response to that (and similar) questions should, in our opinion, be "the photos speak for themselves." In our humble opinions, if the detective answers the question affirmatively, it would appear to the subsequent reader of the transcribed proceedings as though the defendant's photo was made to stand out. If there is an appeal the appellate court will then be forced to view the identification photos used and not rely solely on the transcript.

We point out here that we often tell anyone who will listen that there are two areas where a person can detect a good detective from an exceptional one. They are excellent interrogators (after all a person who can persuade another person to confess to a crime when the authorities have absolutely no evidence and there is no good reason to talk must be good) and they can conduct a proper identification procedure. There can be no harder task than trying

[39] *Foster v California* 394 US 440 (1969)

to assemble a fair and impartial photo or live lineup when you have suspects that are bald, or have pink hair, or wear a patch over one eye, etc.).

Chapter Six
Composite Drawings

Composite images can be beneficial investigative tools. However, they should not be used as stand-alone evidence and composite drawings *do not rise to the level of probable cause*. We suggest that *no one* should ever be arrested or detained based solely on the fact that they resemble or are an exact duplicate of a composite drawing.

The use of composite drawings or images has both positive and negative consequences that should be considered before using them as part of any investigation.

Aggressive solicitation of facial descriptions for a composite drawing may produce a diminished ability to recognize the offender's face at a later time, a phenomenon called verbal overshadowing.[40]   However, in some cases (serial cases for example) a composite image may be the best avenue available to the detective to alert the community through the media.   A composite may also be a good way to alert possible victims and obtain investigative leads.

Composites can provide a depiction that may be used to develop investigative leads. Be aware however, that the quantity and quality of the investigative leads generated may be overwhelming and provide no valuable suspects.

---

[40] Schooler, JW & Engstler-Schooler, TY, *Verbal Overshadowing of Visual Memories: Some Things are Better Left Unsaid.* Cognitive Psychology and Piggott, MA & Brighham, JC. *Relationship Between Accuracy of Prior Description and Facial Recognition.* Journal of Applied Science (1985)

The person preparing the composite should select and employ the composite technique in such a manner that the witness's description is reasonably depicted. The person preparing the composite should assess the physical and mental state of the witness at both the time of the procedure and the time of the incident to determine if any conditions are or were present that could interfere with the witness's ability to give an adequate description of the perpetrator. This choice may be based on the equipment, training, and experience available in each department or jurisdiction.

Showing photos to the witness immediately before a composite procedure could influence the description s/he provides and is not recommended. Multiple witnesses must be separated for composite image procedures.[41]

When the composite is completed, the witness should be informed of how the finished product will be used. If the composite is scheduled to be on television, in the newspaper or displayed in local business establishment windows, the victim and witnesses should know beforehand.

As is true in every identification procedure, documentation of the procedure is essential and required. The person conducting the procedure should preserve the outcome of the procedure by accurately documenting the type of procedure(s) employed and the results. The person conducting the procedure should document the procedure employed (e.g., identikit-type, artist or computer-generated image) in writing. It is a good procedure to have the preparer (artist, computer operator), officer or detective and the witness date and sign the original image. The original composite should, of course, be preserved.

We have mentioned often how important it is for everyone in law enforcement to understand the basics of forensic evidence and investigative techniques and be aware of the benefits and disadvantages of all forensic tests and investigative techniques.

---

[41] ALL identification procedures should be conducted with only one person at a time. ID procedures are NOT joint projects.

For instance, if in a given case, you have a qualified evidence technician take GSR (gunshot residue tests) from a suspect. That sample after forensic testing and evaluation, will, at best, be termed similar and consistent with the fact that the person tested may have been in proximity to a firearm when it was discharged. GSR tests are never positive, are at best, inconclusive and at worst, negative. However, you must remember that many of the negative results are a direct result of some action taken by the suspect (washing hands, wiping hands, sweating while handcuffed and rubbing hands on the transport vehicle's back seat cushions) or time lapse (GSR test results are good usually up to two hours on a live person).

Now, if you are aware of the disadvantages of conducting this forensic procedure, you can then weigh those negatives with the psychological effect it has on a suspect, who may then confess after a test is performed. It is entirely possible that without that GSR test the subject would not have confessed. However, you must also weigh the results of a negative test result when the defense points this out to a jury. You should be prepared to discuss and testify about the problems associated with a GSR test. If you are not prepared or up to date concerning these tests the negatives may well work against you.

In the case of composite drawings, there are two sides to using them also. As we discussed earlier, researchers have found that after a composite drawing has been prepared, the witness may have a problem recognizing the actual offender later, like a lineup or in court.

Although police computer generated composites, foil generated composites and sketch artists rendering of a witness description of a suspect has come under scrutiny in the past several years it is our belief that a composite or artist sketch can still be a valuable investigative tool for the investigating officer. Each case should be evaluated prior to initiating a composite or sketch. Research has shown that even in the best of circumstances with the modern day computerized systems they only have about a 20 percent accuracy rate if they work from a very recent description of the perpetrator. A second critical evaluation must always occur once the sketch or composite is completed, asking the witness how well the final image looks like the perpetrator. If the remark or scale given by the witness is low or below a comfort level for the investigator then the image should not be put out to other investigators or police officers and especially the media. However, if the image is rated high by the witness and fits the original description provided, then strong consideration must be given whether the image should be shown to other investigators and police officers. You would first show the image to the investigators and police officers with the hope that someone may recognize the image as someone they have seen or had contact with in the past. If a suspect is developed from the image then it is imperative to conduct a thorough investigation into this individual to learn whether or not there was motive and opportunity by this suspect. If and only if, no leads have been developed by the release of this image to the police investigators and there is a joint feeling by the investigators and witness that the composite is a very good likeness, should the image then be released to the media.

However, some years back, in Northampton, Massachusetts two victims reported an armed robbery that occurred after attending a show downtown. The victims were brought to the police department where they were interviewed separately. Their versions of the events that evening were consistent up to the point of the actual alleged robbery. Suspicion was drawn from their differing accounts of the event during the robbery and the differences in descriptors of the vehicle and perpetrator. A forensic artist was brought in to attempt to obtain a composite drawing of the suspect. As is proper procedure, each victim was interviewed separately by the artist. After completing one drawing, the artist started fresh with the second victim. To everyone's surprise the second victim described a male black subject as the offender and the first victim had described a male Hispanic offender. Additional investigation provided significant doubt that a crime had actually occurred. The victims, who were in relationships with other people, may have made up the robbery story to cover up a possible domestic confrontation.

Another time in Chicago, a serial rapist had set his sights on the downtown business district. This guy would attack women who arrived for work in the early morning hours. Because of the area the offenses were occurring in, the media was having a field day and the police department was under tremendous pressure to solve the crimes, identify a suspect and arrest the offender. Detectives assigned to the case were able to gain the confidence of one victim. This victim was able to furnish a detailed description to the department's resident forensic artist. Literally thousands of copies of the composite were produced and distributed with the area of the crimes. The media displayed the composite on the late 10 o'clock news and the newspapers were set to publish the suspect's likeness. With no leads generated, detectives in the area of the crimes came up with a plan. Every available detective was told to report for duty the next morning before six o'clock. Each team of two detectives flooded the downtown business area with a stack of Special Bulletins with the offender's composite displayed. The detectives were handing out the bulletins and questioning every pedestrian in the area. Shortly before 8:00 A.M., a male subject approached one team of detectives on a street corner. This male looked at the stack of bulletins in the detective's hand and asked, "Is that my picture from the rapes?" Needless to say the suspect was arrested, identified in several lineups and charged with numerous counts of sexual assault.

In another Northampton, Massachusetts case that Captain Patenaude investigated while still a detective involved a female college student who alleged that she had been raped in a field after leaving her boyfriend's dorm. She claimed to have been sexually assaulted and beaten by the attacker. She displayed signs of scratches and bruising on her face and body. She informed the investigators that she had left her boyfriend's dorm located at another nearby university about seven miles away. As she traveled by way of a short cut back to campus she stopped her car on a very remote back road. She provided the detectives with a description of a white male approximately 6'2" with a muscular build and light colored hair. As a last resort she was requested and agreed to provide a composite image of the perpetrator.

The investigators set up an interview with the boyfriend and agreed to meet outside one of the buildings at his campus. As Detective Patenaude and his supervisor, Sgt. Michael Wall waited for the boyfriend's arrival, Detective Patenaude observed a subject approaching them from a distance and thought he recognized the face. He pulled out the composite and asked Sgt. Wall to confirm his suspicions, which he did. The composite looked strikingly similar to the boyfriend but the physical description did not match, as the boyfriend was maybe 5'7" and was very slim, not muscular. As the investigation continued it became clear that the young woman was not telling us the truth and when presented with the number of discrepancies (not all identified here) the young woman admitted to never having been raped and had inflicted the wounds found on her. After meeting with the parents we learned that their daughter had put an extreme amount of pressure on herself to do well at school that led to this incident. The physical description given fit the father's physique. When completing the composite, the alleged victim had used the two men known best to her to describe her alleged attacker.

There has been some research that suggests that witnesses who create a composite are less accurate at a later recognition of the criminal.[42] Research also shows that it is very difficult to describe a person's facial features because we process faces holistically, not piecemeal.

Most of us don't recognize or recall faces based on their individual features, said Gary Wells, a psychology researcher at Iowa State University who has been active for over twenty years in trying to reform eyewitness identification techniques. Several brain studies have shown that we tend to see a face as a whole and

---

[42] Wells and Hassel (2007)

we pay more attention to the relationship among the parts of a face than we do to the parts themselves. "Every cognitive scientist who has studied faces has concluded that faces are processed holistically. In fact, we now know that at least as early as six months of age, babies are engaged in the holistic processing of faces, not individual features," Dr. Wells said.

"You can take people who've been married 15 or 20 years and the husband or wife can be quite incapable of describing a single feature of the spouse's face accurately," added Christopher Solomon, technical director for a British composite company called VisionMetric Ltd. For that reason, Drs. Wells and Solomon believe most of the computerized composite systems used today have serious flaws.[43]

Additionally, the criminal investigator should remember that the resulting composite is not always realistic or similar in appearance to the criminal. The lesson here is to always be aware of the plus and negative sides of every investigative and forensic technique utilized.

---

[43] Mark Roth "*Why police composites don't always hit mark*", *New system for police sketches takes into consideration that witnesses typically recall the entire face, not individual features*, Sunday, March 25, 2007, Pittsburgh Post-Gazette)

Chapter 7
Pre-Identification
Instructions to the Witness

As we noted in the introduction, a great number of positive changes have occurred in the field of eyewitness identification since the October 1999 publication of *Eyewitness Evidence, a Guide for Law Enforcement*. The Technical Working Group for Eyewitness Evidence (TWGEYEE) members added one new eyewitness instruction to be provided by police when a victim/ witness views an identification procedure. That instruction was that regardless of whether an identification is made, the police will continue to investigate the incident. TWGEYEE members felt that the addition of this instruction would further relieve the pressure that a victim/witness feels to make an identification, even if they weren't positive about their identification. It appears, from our limited research, that a large number of states and law enforcement agencies have adopted this instruction or now have similar wording in their victim/witness identification instructions and that now appears to be a standard practice.[44]

The reasons for eyewitness unreliability are numerous and caused by any number of factors and circumstances. The fact that police are showing a lineup to a witness will lead some witnesses to presume that the actual perpetrator will be in the lineup and that their only job is to make an identification. This is certainly the case when an investigator contacts a victim or witness and states to

[44] *Eyewitness Evidence, a Guide for Law Enforcement*, page 32

them "We have arrested the person who robbed you. I'd like to come by and see if you can identify him." The use of instructions is intended to, at least, reduce those assumptions.

There are those factors at a crime scene that no one has any control over such as; amount of lighting, the distance between perpetrator and witness, witness stress level, attention deficit, weapon focus, and age to name just a few (circumstances that researchers call estimator variables). However, there are factors that law enforcement can control (referred to as system variables by the research community) and that starts with the preservation of the eyewitness evidence as if you would a murder weapon. With a murder weapon, you examine it, tag it, bag it, and send it to the crime laboratory experts for examination and wait for the results. Eyewitness evidence is critical evidence that may be the only evidence you have available. It too must be preserved, gathered and examined for reliability and credibility like any physical evidence you may process at a crime scene.

The witness should not be told anything that might influence his/her decision to choose a photo, or person such as the fact that the individuals portrayed have arrest records, the offenses for which the individuals were arrested, or the geographical area with which they are associated. This is important to help the witness not feel pressured to make a selection.

Informing the witness of identification procedure instructions is vital and can be the difference between picking a filler (innocent person) and not selecting anyone because the actual perpetrator is not within the group of individuals or photographs/images presented. It also offers the witness another option to the multiple choice question inferred when s/he is asked if they recognize anyone in the lineup. The traditional answer to this multiple answer question is to select from one of the 6 or 8 photographs/ persons presented. Proper instructions allow for the "none of the above" choice to this question.

Witnesses may recognize a photo or suspect for reasons other than it being a photo of the perpetrator. Therefore, it is important to determine how or from where the witness knows the depicted individual. For example, the witness may recognize someone he/she just saw in the precinct lobby.

Providing instructions to the witness can improve his/her comfort level and can result in information that may assist the investigation.

We agree that instruction given prior to ANY identification procedure is essential for a fair and reliable identification procedure.

One of the current instructions, i.e.; that the persons presented in the identification procedure may have changed in appearance since the incident, is under scrutiny. Some researchers have suggested that this instruction does not help the witness and may be responsible for filler picks. Some feel that the use of this particular instruction essentially suggests to the witness that the suspect has somehow changed his appearance and keys the witness to look for this alleged change. It seems to us that it is possible this instruction may only be given when the suspect has changed his appearance (by shaving or coloring his hair, etc) and will not be given when no obvious changes have been made. We also feel that a positive identification of a suspect, after he has changed his appearance is a stronger identification. Take for instance where a witness states "it's number two, but he cut his hair" or "it's number four, but he shaved off his mustache." We remind our readers that it is essential to use the same identical instructions when conducting every identification procedure. This will ensure that when testifying in court the officer is able to say that these instructions are used in every case, not just when a suspect has changed his appearance or that the instruction is never used.

The following are the instructions commonly believed to contain the essential spirit of the lineup instructions and a further explanation for instructions, where required to clarify its intent.

1-I am going to show you a group of photographs/images/individuals.

2-The photographs/images/individuals are in a random order.

3-These photographs/images/individuals will be viewed one at a time.

4-You can take as much time as you need to make a decision about each one before moving to the next.

5-The person who committed the crime may or may not be in the lineup.

Some studies[45] reveal that the use of just this one instruction, the possible absence of the actual perpetrator/offender, reduces the frequency of picking a filler by up to 42% when the actual offender is not present in the identification procedure.

6-It is just as important to clear innocent persons from suspicion as it is to identify the guilty person. This instructions helps emphasize that failure to identify anyone, might be the appropriate outcome.

7-Individuals in the lineup may not appear exactly as they did at the time of the incident.[46]

One study indicates that this instruction did not increase offender identifications & reduced confidence. The important thing to remember here is that if you employ this instruction, it should be employed in every case, not just in cases where the suspect's appearance has changed. Also, if you or your department chooses not to use this instruction, it should not be used for any identification procedures. It is important to be consistent.

8-If you do not make an identification the police will continue to investigate the case.

This instruction is intended to further relieve pressure on the witness to make an identification.

9-If you make an identification, the procedure requires that you indicate in your own words how certain you are of the identification.

---

[45] Steblay, N. (1997). *Social influence in eyewitness recall: A meta-analytic review of line-up instruction effects.* Law and Human Behavior , 21, 283-297.

[46] see Charman and Wells *Eyewitness Lineups: Is the Appearance Change Instruction a Good Idea?*, 2005

The only time the witness's certainty is believed to be accurate is at the time of an identification, prior to any feedback or other outside influences.

10-All photos/persons will be shown, even if an identification is made; or the procedure will be stopped at the point of an identification (consistent with jurisdictional/departmental procedures).

The administrator should follow a fixed technique (or the law enforcement agency should have a formal written policy) as to whether the procedure will stop when the witness makes a selection of a photo or whether the procedure will continue until all photos are presented. If the investigator sometimes continues to show photos and sometimes does not, it could appear that the decision to continue is being based on whether the witness is making the right pick.

11-Do not indicate to any other witness that you have or have not made an identification.

Obviously, for fair procedures, others who are involved should not have any knowledge of the identification.

The instruction stated here, that all photos will be shown even if the witness identifies the perpetrator before they complete the process and look at all of the images or individuals, is important. If the first photo is the perpetrator and identified by the witness without looking at all of the images/individuals, in some jurisdictions, that may be considered a show-up and assuredly a defense attorney will file a motion indicating such. In other jurisdictions appellate courts have ruled that if the number one photo was truly random (as in shuffling), that would be allowed.

Investigators are also reminded that everything that occurs during a criminal investigation is likely to be challenged. We maintain your investigation is only as good as it can be presented in a court of law. Always consider your case from the point of view of a defense attorney or as the devil's advocate and anticipate what holes they may see in your case and plug them no matter how insignificant the hole or interview may seem.

If the identification procedure administrator stops a lineup after an identification, it may indicate to that detective how strong that identification is. However, the defense is likely to file a motion to suppress that identification stating the witness didn't give the procedure a fair chance; he only looked at two photos. If however, the lineup administrator continues until all the images have been viewed before soliciting a selection from the witness, the defense attorney is now just as likely to file a motion to suppress any identification that states if the witness really recognized number two as the offender, why didn't the police stop the lineup then?

If your department has a contemporary formal written policy stating its preference (show all images or photographs or persons even if an identification has been made or stop the procedure when and identification is obtained), the officer can testify in court as to the reason for either stopping the procedure or completing the procedure after an identification.

Another issue that has come about was during an actual Northampton, Massachusetts Police Department burglary case where the homeowner confronted the perpetrator inside his home before the perpetrator fled. The homeowner was brought to the police department to view a sequential photo lineup with a blind administrator. During this procedure the witness stated, as he looked at image #2, "That may be him." The officer continued the procedure and continued to view the rest of the images. When shown the fourth photograph, the witness exclaimed that, "No that's him, that's definitely him, that's the guy."

A point worthy of notation here is why the witness initially picked #2. After review of the lineup it was clear that #2 looked a lot like the perpetrator. Fillers that are similar to the suspect or meet the general description given by the witness of the suspect are selected by the investigators so that the suspect does not unduly stand out.

Consider if you will, that with the use of a blind administrator and random positioning of the suspects, if the identification procedure is stopped at the time of an ID and that identification is of a filler, the actual offender would never be observed, not to mention identified.

The reader can clearly see why we prefer showing all the subjects in the lineup.

Recommended Instructions for most identification procedures may be found in Chapter 14 on Forms and Procedural Orders later in this publication.

Chapter 8
Conducting Show-Ups

One of the greatest tools in any first responder's investigative tool box is the show-up. It is also one the most misunderstood procedures employed by police officials. We, however, are acutely aware of the inherent suggestiveness of the show-up procedure. We also understand that this type of identification procedure is widely misunderstood, and possibly misused, by some law enforcement officers.

One of the reasons that we believe in the use of show-ups (within the judicial guidelines established) rests on the facts that a show-up is both timely and the suspect is presented live. This affords the witness an opportunity to view the suspect, his height, clothing and mannerisms immediately following the crime. A show-up allows a witness to view a suspect while the witness's memory is fresh, which minimizes the chance of mistaken identification.[47] The show-up also has the benefit of being easy to arrange, which promotes efficient police work by enabling officers to quickly determine whether they have detained the perpetrator or an innocent suspect.[48]

Defense attorneys and some legal scholars seem to believe that whenever a show up is conducted by a law enforcement official, the victim or witness will automatically pick the detained person just because he is in close proximity to the police. We would like

[47] See *Commonwealth v. Crowley*, 29 Mass. App. Ct.1 (1990)

[48] See *Simmons v. U.S.*, 390 U.S. 377 (1968)

74

to remind the reader that these defense attorneys and researchers have never been there, at three o'clock in the morning, when a victim tells an officer or deputy sheriff "that's not the guy who robbed me"! Practical experience (and understanding of the relevant appellate court decisions, through training or research), we believe, with show-ups is a better teacher than guesses or assumptions.

However, you must be careful because you may have a rare case where a witness may identify an individual just for the fact that the police have him detained. There was a case that occurred in Florida that was shared with us by a student during a break in the class. This student (Hillsborough County Sheriff) informed us that they had stopped a young man for a sexual assault one evening and brought the victim to the location where the officers had the individual detained and she identified him as the perpetrator. When his alibi was checked out and was considered a concrete alibi the student had questioned the victim how she had come to identify this individual and she stated to him "that because you (the police) had stopped him so it must have been him." We stress the importance of proper instructions to victims/witnesses prior to any identification process including show-ups!

During our eyewitness evidence training sessions, we use a short video segment taken from the full length feature film, *The Hurricane*. For the reader unfamiliar with the film or the segment referred to, we offer the following scenario: A tavern is robbed late at night during which several patrons are shot and killed by two males who flee in a beige Dodge vehicle. Subsequently, officers who were conducting a systematic search of the area come across a beige Dodge vehicle. The vehicle and the occupants fit the descriptions furnished by one of the victims. The vehicle is within a reasonable distance from the robbery and murder location within a short time after the offense. Officers stop the suspect vehicle and identify the two occupants. The two occupants are taken to the hospital where the only known living witness is undergoing a medical procedure in the emergency room. The officers ask the doctor for and receive permission to speak with the injured (shot) victim. The two suspects are brought in to the room where the victim is lying, bleeding, with tubes attached to his arms. The victim is then asked "are these the two men that did it sir"?

The following questions are then asked of the class; "what do you think of this identification procedure" and "would you consider using this type of procedure"? These two questions are often answered by some law enforcement personnel with laughter or outright scorn. Comments run from "you can't do that!" to "you must be kidding, that's not legal"! To the less experienced or under educated officers, this particular case example appears to be a bad or even sinister abuse of power. Some officers also state defense type objections to the procedure such as; the victim is under the influence of drugs after being shot. (In the movie clip shown, the victim indicates that these two are not the persons that shot him.)

How is it that the defense oriented class members know that this type of show-up example, while extreme, falls within realm of legality and admissible evidence?

One explanation in support of the show-up is the conservative approach that states evidence that is not obtained cannot be suppressed. While that seems an extreme statement, let's consider the facts as stated in this example. We have a victim close to death and the other known victims are deceased in a brutal robbery murder. We know of no other witnesses. What could be considered more exigent than this? The reader is also asked to remember that we are not seeking to charge and convict the suspects (if they are identified), we are attempting to either obtain probable cause to detain or arrest them or release these suspects and continue to seek the actual offenders. Let us not forget that we work just as hard to exonerate as we do to convict. Further evidence of the value and reliability of the show-up procedure comes from the Massachusetts District Attorney's Association (MDAA). That organization conducted a study of fifteen years of erroneous convictions and reported that there was no erroneous conviction cases in Boston based on an inaccurate show-up identification, which provides some anecdotal evidence for the reliability of show-up identifications.[49]

To explain, let's examine the principal behind the show-up identification procedure. First, what is a show-up? It is a one on one showing of a suspect that generally fits the description of a wanted offender who is stopped and detained within a reasonable time and distance from the scene of a crime. The stop of the subject must be reasonable, i.e.: a male matching the physical and clothing description of a wanted person walking three blocks from the scene within a few minutes of the crime would be reasonable. That person walking three miles from the crime scene two minutes after the incident probably wouldn't be reasonable.

There are, however, exceptions allowed by our courts. Remember that every criminal case and investigative technique should be evaluated separately considering known facts and circumstances. Take for example, this robbery shooting case from Chicago that Sgt. Carroll investigated:

At about 7:00 P.M. on a warm summer evening a group of men were participating in an illegal dice game on the third floor of one of the city's many housing project buildings. An unknown subject came out of the nearby stairwell waving a handgun. This subject demanded money from the players. One of the participants apparently was slow in delivering his money and was shot in the neck. Everyone fled the scene prior to the arrival of the police except the victim. The victim was transported to a local trauma center where it was determined that his spinal cord had been severed. The investigation quickly focused on occupants of the building where the crime had occurred. After several suspects were eliminated over several months of investigation, a former occupant of the building was identified as a suspect. A photo lineup was prepared and the victim identified the suspect as the

---

[49] Report of the Justice Initiative, Recommendations of the Massachusetts Attorney General and the District Attorneys to Improve the Investigation & prosecution of Cases in the Criminal Justice Systems, September 2006.

person that had robbed and shot him. This suspect was apprehended, but with only a photo identification, the prosecutor's office declined to charge him. We note here, that due to his injuries, the victim was still in a rehabilitation institute paralyzed from the neck down. Illinois courts are adamant in their preference for live identifications of suspects. During his tenure with the Chicago Police Department's Detective Division (almost twenty years) Sgt. Carroll was never allowed by the State's Attorneys Office to charge a suspect without a live lineup identification. Added to this, the rehabilitation institute refused to allow a full five person live lineup to be conducted in their facility. After additional talks with the prosecutor's office, it was decided to have a show-up at the institute where the victim was confined. Not only was the suspect identified again, he broke down and tearfully confessed to the crime. He was subsequently sentenced to a long prison sentence.[50]

Show-ups are not group projects. If there is more than one witness or victim of a crime, only one person should view the detained suspect. Further, if an identification is obtained of this subject from the first witness, it is best to conduct any additional identification procedures at a different place and in a different manner, i.e.; photo lineup, live lineup, etc. The U.S. Supreme Court has stated that the reliability of an identification procedure can be enhanced by using a photo array with one or two witnesses and, if an identification is made, using a (live) lineup for other witnesses.[51] Some jurisdictions, notably Wisconsin, restrict show-ups by requiring a physical arrest if probable cause exists and an identification procedure other than a show-up be used.[52]

---

[50] Also see *Commonwealth v. Cox*, 6 Mass. App. Ct. 968 (1979)

[51] See *Simmons v. United States*, 390 U.S. 377 (1968)

[52] *State of Wisconsin v Dubose*, 7/14/2005

Every identification procedure, positive or negative, including show-ups requires a lineup report.[53]

The justification for show-ups is recognized by our courts due to exigent (requiring immediate action) circumstances. The courts recognize the duty of the police to investigate criminal activity. The judges reason that it is necessary to conduct detentions to further this endeavor. A pat down search may also be allowed if the circumstances warrant additional intrusion to the stopped subject, i.e.; wanted suspect is armed and a bulge is noticeable in the subject's pocket or for the officer's safety if s/he feels threatened). The police must be able to apprehend the responsible party and quickly release those determined not to be involved. This will enable the police to continue their search for the actual perpetrator.

The courts, however, are well aware that while a show-up can provide investigative leads at an early stage in the investigation, the inherent suggestiveness requires careful use of procedural safeguards. Investigators recognize the value of the procedure because the suspect is stopped within the immediate area of the crime within a short time after the crime and that after an arrest based on a positive identification, any evidence of the crime found during a search of the suspect (proceeds or weapon) will enhance the prosecution and almost guarantee a conviction.

To better explain the concept of the show-up we submit to the reader the following example of what a legally admissible show-up would be:

Car 101 is assigned to a radiogram of a Robbery Just Occurred at the Stop & Rob located at 1234 S. Main Street, the offender described as a male white, 18 to 21 years of age, 6 feet tall, brown hair, wearing blue jeans and an orange T-shirt. Car 101 continues to the scene, while looking for suspects fleeing the area. The officer(s) arrives, notes that the suspect has fled (if this is the case, no additional units are needed and should be directed to systematically search the area and secure probable escape routes),

---

[53] See chapter on Documentation

secures, protects and preserves the crime scene. The victim's needs are assessed and first aid rendered (if required). The type of crime is determined and an updated description of the suspect is broadcast to all cars, including the type or absence of any weapons observed (we want all responding units to know this information both for safety and operational reasons, after all we don't want to shoot an unarmed shoplifter, but we want to be safe at the same time).

Assisting patrol units are conducting a systematic search of the area (not responding to the crime scene, unless specifically requested by the assigned unit) or are positioned at logical escape routes (highway ramps, major thoroughfares, etc.). Unit 102 observes a suspect who matches the description of the wanted offender four blocks from the scene. The officer stops the subject and inquires as to the subject's reason for being in the area. The officer then notifies the handling unit (Car 101) that s/he has a subject detained and gives the officer his location. Car 101 escorts the victim to the scene of the detention (in route the officer reads the victim show-up instructions[54]) where a positive identification is made (the victim screams "THAT'S THE GUY WHO ROBBED ME"! The subject is then arrested and a search of his person incident to the arrest yields identifiable property taken in the robbery and the proceeds from the crime.

In a perfect world (where sufficient patrol personnel are available), Car 101 completes his preliminary investigation at the original scene and reports his investigation on the original offense report. Car 102 effects the arrest of the suspect and prepares a supplemental report detailing his part in the investigation, including the stop, detention, show-up, identification, arrest and search of the arrestee. If there is limited personnel available for proper coverage of the area, Car 102 can place his arrest in a cell and resume patrol pending completion of Car 101s preliminary investigation, including processing of the scene for evidence, including photographs.

---

[54] Refer to chapter 7 on instructions

If however, Car 102s street stop results in no identification, that fact should be reported either with the preparation of a supplemental report which includes the subject's name and identifiers or the information regarding the subject can be included in Car 101s original report.

Returning to the original example at the hospital, the only difference with the two described cases is that in one case, the stopped subject is taken to another (herein the hospital) location for the show-up. We do however, remind the reader that it is preferable to bring the victim or witness to the stopped subject. Taking the stopped subject to the crime scene is not advisable as it opens the procedure to legal motions to suppress evidence in court. Notably, was the defendant in custody? Another defense motion (or questioning in court) might take the following form: "Of course you found my client's fingerprints or DNA at the scene officer. After all, you brought him back there didn't you"?

The law and court decisions regarding all types of identification procedures are under attack more than ever. Because we recognize that show-ups are, by the very nature of the procedure, inherently suggestive (but we believe not *unnecessarily suggestive*), we recommend the following procedures:

1-Prior to any show-up, obtain and document or record the description of the wanted suspect.

2-If a stop is made; it is preferable to bring the witness to the detained suspect.

3-If multiple witnesses are involved, separate the witnesses and instruct them to avoid discussing the details of the incident.

4-Choose the best witness to view the stopped subject.

5-Review with the witness instructions for show-up procedures.[55]

6-If an identification is obtained; consider using other identification procedures (live lineup or photo array) for the additional witnesses.

---

[55] Refer to chapter on instructions prior to identification procedures Ch 7 in this publication

7-Document every identification procedure.

8-Obtain a statement of certainty from the witness.[56]

When circumstances require the prompt display of a single suspect to a witness, challenges to the inherent suggestiveness of the encounter can be minimized through the use of proper procedural safeguards. The investigator should use procedures that avoid unnecessary suggestiveness.

We also remind the reader that some appellate courts have ruled that when probable cause to arrest exists, no show-up should be conducted. The suspect should be arrested and another type of identification procedure should be held.[57]   Show ups at a law enforcement facility should be avoided.

We believe that show ups, when properly conducted, are a valuable asset to law enforcement and the citizens they serve. We understand the opposition to the procedure from researchers, scholars and defense attorneys and agree with these professions that a show up is a highly suggestive procedure. We also know that if a show up is conducted with proper safeguards and in compliance with court decisions/guidelines, the show-up may well yield corroborative evidence, i.e.; proceeds from the offense, or the weapon used to commit the offense. The show-up may well ensure that the right offender is subsequently prosecuted and the innocent suspect freed without delay.

If the right to conduct show-ups is taken away from police officers, the only alternative remaining for the officer or deputy is to arrest the subject or release a possible guilty person. We can only imagine what the courts would do in this situation, not to mention the added burden to those arrested and to the police or sheriff's department involved.

We believe strongly about the proper use of the show up. Because of their awareness of current challenges to the show-up

---

[56] Refer to certainty statements later in this publication

[57] See *State v. Dubose* 285 Wis.2d, 143 (2005)

procedure, we have made and distributed an instruction card to our students at our training sessions.

Researchers and other scholars, without real life law enforcement operational experience, tend to see only the clinical issues involved. Indeed, a few years ago a well respected researcher contacted one of us and asked why, instead of a show up, the police couldn't just take a suspect to a police facility or substation and take his photo (digital image) for use in a lineup procedure. This researcher fails to understand that this suspect may well refuse to go to the police facility as well as decline to have his photograph taken and that he is well within his rights to do so.

Another time, while meeting with several of the research experts, it was suggested that technology now exists where if a suspect was observed and stopped by the police, the officer could obtain the suspect's name and identifying information. This information could be entered into the vehicle computer and a digital image obtained. The researchers believe that if this image matched the suspect, a data base could be searched and a photo line p could be prepared and then shown to the witness.

In theory, in the near future, this capability may be available in some jurisdictions and holds some promise. On an operational level, however, who would watch the suspect who has not been arrested while the officer conducts this computer inquiry?[58] What happens if the suspect, as is his constitutional right, declines to identify himself?

---

[58] See A. Murgard *Best Practices, The Threat of Technology* Police Magazine, Vol. 35, No 7, , July, 2011

Chapter 9
Sequential Procedures:
Preventing Relative Judgment

We were both somewhat skeptical when first introduced to the sequential identification procedures, but after extensive review of the research (especially that on human memory and relative judgments) we both feel STRONGLY that sequential procedures are superior to the old simultaneous identification procedures where all the suspects are shown at the same time. When coupled with double blind procedures and proper instructions (discussed later in this publication) the results of sequential identification procedure is much stronger evidence in court.

The sequential procedure is meant to reduce the tendency of the witness to compare one photo with another photo (i.e., make relative judgments). The idea is for the witness to make a decision on each image/person by comparing the particular image/person with that of their memory of the perpetrator before moving on to view the next image or person. The sequential procedure is designed to reduce the witness's reliance on relative judgments or process of elimination process thereby eliminating "which one should I pick?"

The sequential procedure was first proposed in 1985 (Professors Lindsay & Wells) as a way to encourage a comparison to a memory, not to other photos or persons.

The Northampton Police Department implemented their first eyewitness evidence policy that was based upon the Department Of Justice Guide that included both simultaneous and sequential methods of photo array presentation. The implementation of the new policy was accompanied by a 2 hour training program to all police personnel. Over a period of approximately twelve months, as the Detective Bureau Commander, then Lt. Ken Patenaude observed that the investigators were using the sequential double blind procedures almost exclusively. The detectives had been given a choice as to the type of identification procedure to employ between simultaneous and sequential. When the Northampton detectives were questioned why they preferred the change to the sequential method over the long standing simultaneous method they cited four very important reasons. First, the detectives stated that they were more confident in the witness identifications they were obtaining from the sequential method because they felt it was a test of the witness's memory versus a simultaneous method. Second, after some growing pains they were comfortable with the blind administration and felt it would eliminate any inadvertent cues, thus less defense council motions. Third, they were confident they could explain the methodology behind the sequential double blind procedures to a jury or to the court, and forth, they felt that the sequential procedure would reduce the chances of a misidentification. As a result of the DNA exonerations, the Social Science Research findings and the detective's remarks, in 2002-2003 the Northampton Police Department changed their eyewitness identification policy that mandated sequential double blind lineup and photo array procedures.

Several years had passed and only three motions had been filed related to the identification process, none of which involved the new procedural methods; the motions were related to the photos employed. The sequential double blind procedures are still being implemented ten years later with confidence these are the best eyewitness identification practices.

Research shows that eyewitnesses tend to select the person who looks most like the perpetrator relative to the other lineup members. This fact is not a problem in the vast majority of criminal cases when the actual offender is present in the lineup shown or when the police have overwhelming corroborative evidence. Relative judgment becomes a very serious problem and can lead to erroneous convictions when the actual offender is not present. Of the 280 erroneous criminal convictions overturned to date using DNA evidence, the actual offender was not present in the actual identification procedure. In spite of this, a suspect was identified, convicted and the conviction upheld on appeal until DNA technology was applied to the case.

Relative judgment is analogous to a multiple choice test that we are all familiar with, without the "none of the above" answer. The fact that police are showing a lineup can lead some witnesses to presume that the actual perpetrator is in the lineup. The witness picks the best (most correct) answer in relation to the question asked, or in the case of an identification procedure, the suspect that looks closest to the offender. The sequential procedure along with the use of instructions can help eliminate this assumption.

In 1993, Professor Gary Wells, Ph.D. from Iowa State University and widely considered the leading expert on eyewitness identification research, conducted an experiment using the removal without replacement procedure that in essence explains how relative judgment occurs. Professor Wells held a staged crime for 200 eyewitnesses who were later shown a lineup. Half (or 100) people were shown a six pack lineup that contained the suspect and the other 100 people were shown the same lineup, except that the actual offender was removed. In Professor Wells' experiment all of the 200 eyewitnesses were told that the actual culprit may or may not be present.

The results of the first lineup revealed that 54% picked the actual offender, 21% failed to make a choice, 13% chose a filler and the four remaining fillers each received 3%. The results of the second lineup procedure, where the actual offender was removed, surprised everyone.

Most of us would expect that with the actual offender removed from the lineup, leaving only five fillers, the no choice option would absorb the real offender's numbers and increase to 75%.

The results revealed the following: The four fillers that had originally received 3% of the picks each, now increased to 5%, 6%, 7% and 12%. The no choice group went up, but only to 32%. The remaining filler now received 38% of the identifications, an increase of 25%.[59]

The relative judgment process helps us to understand the importance of instructions regarding the possible absence of the perpetrator, the best strategies for selecting lineup fillers (discussed later) and the greater time to decision associated with mistaken identifications.

Recognition memory is largely automatic, rapid, and nonverbal while the relative judgment process is more deliberate, effortful and nonverbal "It just popped out."[60]   The relative judgment process is more deliberate, effortful and verbal. "I first tried to decide which person displayed could not be the guy. Just like the penny memory display discussed earlier."   The sequential eyewitness identification procedure is designed to make eyewitness identification more reliable by preventing witnesses from merely making relative judgments.

A major difference between the simultaneous and sequential procedure is that the sequential procedure attempts to prevent the eyewitness from merely making relative judgments.   Readers should be aware that relative judgments can be problematic because they involve comparing one lineup member to another and picking the person who most looks like the perpetrator.   The sequential procedure leads witnesses to compare each lineup member with their memory of the perpetrator rather than comparing one lineup member with another. The problem with the relative judgment process is that some member in the identification procedure will always look more like the offender than the

---

59 Gary L. Wells, Mark Small, Steven Penrod, Roy Malpass, Solomon M.
    Fulero, and C.A. Brimacombe *Eyewitness Identification Procedures:
    Recommendations for Lineups and Photospreads* Law and Human
    Behavior, Vol.22, No.6, 1998,

60 Dunning, 1994; Robinson, & Johnson & Herndon, 1997; Sporer, 1992-93-94;
    Wells, 1999

remaining members, even when the actual perpetrator is not in the lineup.

Extensive research has shown that the sequential presentation method reduces rates of mistaken identification without significant harm to accurate identification rates.

The sequential procedure has been studied and replicated outside of United States in many countries, including; Canada, Australia, New Zealand, Japan, Israel, Germany, South Africa and the United Kingdom.

That is not to say that you or your agency may not get fewer eyewitness identifications when using sequential procedures. In fact, one study suggests that there may be a 15% loss of identifications.[61]   However, it is virtually impossible to compare year to year numbers to determine if there is a loss of actual offender picks, more or fewer incidents requiring fewer or more lineups, or poorer witnesses.   Also, fewer picks using the sequential method may simply be a strong indication that the witness is unable to make a selection based on their memory or lack there of.

---

[61] Report to the Legislature of the State of Illinois at www.chicagopolice.org/IL %20Pilot%20on%20eyewitness%20ID.pdff

Chapter 10
Witness Bolstering & Certainty Statement

While our courts have long frowned on the police leading witnesses toward a particular member of the lineup, the courts have shown profound indifference to what police might say to the witness after an identification. Comments like "Yes! You got him!" or "Good, you identified the suspect" or even applauding after an identification of the suspect are common.

Most of us are probably not aware of how influential an officer's comments are to a witness after an identification procedure when a suspect has been identified. Officers have been made acutely aware of contamination from other witnesses and have been trained to go to great lengths to keep witnesses separated before and after identification procedures. Research had not been used by police investigators until recently (the last ten years or so) concerning officer feedback to a witness, known as witness bolstering. Indeed, some officers known to us felt that an encouraging comment from them to the witness after an identification procedure helped to ease the witness' stress due to the identification procedure and investigation.

These officers were unaware of the dramatic effect even these small comments had on the confidence of the witness after an identification was made. We are aware that by the time a criminal case reaches a court room almost every witness is extremely confident in his or her identification of the suspect (now defendant) sitting at the defense table. Testimony elicited by both the prosecution and the defense at this time very often results in testimony similar to" I'll never forget that face" or "I'm one hundred percent that he is the person that did this to me"!

During the early sessions of the U.S. Department of Justice, National Institute of Justice, Technical Working Group on Eyewitness Evidence, the researchers expressed a desire that after an identification procedure, the victim and witnesses not be informed whether the person they identified was the actual suspect or if, s/he would be charged with a crime.

Naturally, the law enforcement members of the group were more than a little surprised at this comment. In our world there were no conceivable circumstances where it was even remotely possible to avoid letting the victim know they had identified the offender or perpetrator. Even if the officer or detective made no comment at all after the identification procedure, a prosecutor would (in some jurisdictions) interview the witness and evaluate the case. It is possible that a sworn criminal complaint may need to be signed. The media might pick up the case to inform the public that a dangerous predator had been taken into custody or any number of other issues could arise making it virtually impossible not to let the victim know the actual identification results.

The entire criminal justice system is also acutely aware that, in a court of law, there is no stronger evidence than a witness pointing to the defendant from the witness box and uttering the words "that's the guy"!

Another instruction adopted by TWGEYEE members was the requirement for the official conducting the lineup or show up to obtain a "Statement of Certainty" from the person viewing the identification procedure prior to any comment or feedback from the officer conducting the procedure.

On its face, this seems rather silly. Obtaining this kind of statement had always been an important part of the identification procedure, hadn't it? After all, a victim or witness had to be sure whenever a suspect was identified in any identification procedure.

It was the researcher's position that the victim or witness should never be informed that they had identified a person that the police and prosecutor would subsequently charge with the crime under investigation. Research had long ago revealed that once the victim had been told that they had picked the right guy their confidence literally soared. It was obvious to the law enforcement personnel and the defense representatives that the victim or witness was entitled to some feedback regarding their participation in the identification procedure. The police officials had to find a compromise that would satisfy not only themselves and their understanding of criminal justice proceedings, but the fears of the researchers as well. It was decided that no comments of any kind would be forthcoming until after a statement of certainty was obtained from the victim or witness. The statement was to be memorialized verbatim. This simple change satisfied both the scientific evidence and the real life problems faced by those involved in the criminal case.

We now know that witness confidence is about the only aspect of an identification that jurors consider.[62] In one study, without eyewitness evidence in a mock jury trial, the conviction rate was 18%. The addition of an eyewitness identification increased the conviction rate to 72% and even when the eyewitness identification was impeached, the guilty rate was still 68%.[63]

Extensive research has revealed that the slightest confirmation to a witness that they identified the right or correct suspect affects the way that the witness feels about their identification and indeed affects the way they remember the suspect.

Professor Gary Wells, Ph.D., from Iowa State University, made the results of his extensive research regarding witness bolstering most understandable while appearing on a Dateline, NBC television program in July of 2010. During the broadcast Dr. Wells

---

[62] Loftus, E. & Doyle, J. Eyewitness Testimony: Civil and Criminal (Lexis Law Publishing, 3rd ed.; 1997)

[63] Cutler, B., Penrod, S. & Dexter, H. *Juror Sensitivity to Eyewitness Identification Evidence.* Law and Human Behavior 12, 41-56

explained how he uses a poorly taped segment depicting a person planting a bomb on the roof of a building. He then conducts lineups with the audience that viewed this tape. One half of the audience is told they made the correct identification and the other half of the audience is given no feedback. Sometime later he asks the audience questions about the crime to gauge their responses. The results of those questionnaires are sobering. The group that was given no feedback was unsure of their identifications and admitted that they didn't get a good look at the suspect. Those that were told that they had correctly identified the offender stated that they were able to get a good look at the suspect and were very confident in their identification of that suspect!

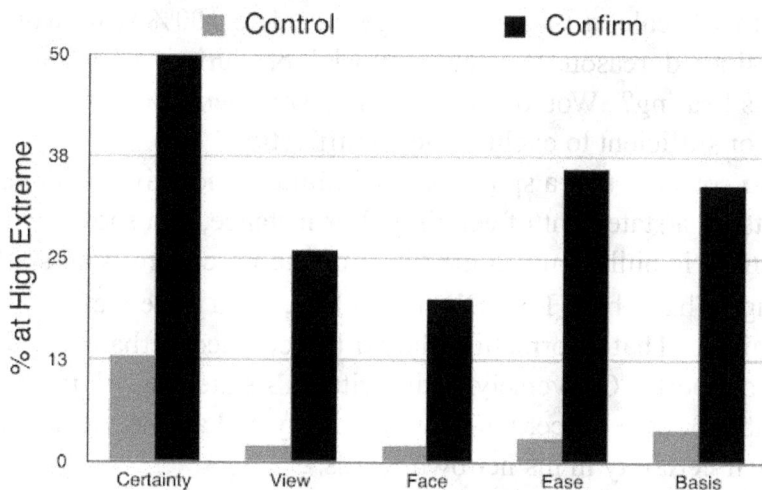

Courtesy of Professor Gary Wells, Iowa State University

With information concerning this type of research, and our practical field experience, we highly recommend obtaining a statement of certainty from every witness after s/he views any identification procedure. This statement must be obtained before any other conversation.

Instructions concerning obtaining a certainty statement should be given to every witness before any identification procedure. This should be done as part of the overall instruction process (see chapter on Instructions). Advise the witness that the identification procedure requires the investigator to ask the witness to state, in his/or her own words, how certain he/or she is of any identification. It is important that the witness understands that the investigator is not questioning the witness's choice or their certainty. If the instruction is not given, the witness may feel that the investigator is questioning the witness's choice. It is preferred that the witness not give a number to express his/or her certainty. Consider that some people will never use the number 10 on a one to ten scale; some may be reluctant to use 100% on a 1 to 100 scale, even though they may be absolutely positive of their identification. The problem comes down to understanding exactly what the witness is trying to express. Consider also, what number on a 1 to 10 scale or what percentage on a 1 to 100% scale would be considered reasonable doubt at trial or during a motion to suppress hearing? Would a 9 or 92% be sufficient for a not guilty verdict or sufficient to exclude the identification?

Also consider that a spontaneous definite or negative statement is, by itself, a statement of certainty. For instance, at a show-up, as the witness is pulling up to the place of the procedure, s/he starts shouting "That's him, I KNOW that's him," you have a statement of certainty. That information should be recorded verbatim in the officer's report. Conversely, if the witness's statement is" it could be number 3," the officer will want to clarify and ask the witness to state their certainty in his/her own words.

If an identification is made, avoid reporting to the witness any information regarding the individual s/he has selected before obtaining any witness's statement of certainty. If the investigator wants to question the witness about certainty, the witness should not be told anything about the status of the person identified at this point (e.g., do not say, that is the person we have as a suspect, or that is the same person that another witness picked; do not say anything that discounts the witness's selection, such as, that person is not a suspect.) This includes nonverbal reactions, such as facial expressions when the witness expresses in his/her choice.

The statement of certainty obtained at the time of the identification, prior to any feedback or any comment from the investigator and properly recorded, is the only time that the witness's opinion concerning the identification is reliable.

Chapter 11
Double Blind Administration

One of best ways to avoid witness bolstering is to have a law enforcement official *who is not familiar with the facts or circumstances surrounding the case* administer the lineup procedure.

An investigator can give inadvertent cues to a witness without realizing it. Examples of inadvertent verbal cues are; The suspect is in position #3 and the witness says, "um....#2" and the response from the investigator is, "be sure you look at everyone" which gives the witness the impression it is not #2, or the witness says, "um...#3" and the investigators response is," tell me about #3", which may suggest to the witness that's the right selection or the witness says nothing and the investigator says to the witness "I noticed you paused at #3 is there something about #3" which is another indication by the investigator that #3 is the correct choice.

When this idea that the investigator assigned to the case shouldn't conduct his/her own identification procedures was first proposed to the group (by the researchers at one of the early TWG meetings during 1999), we were shocked and insulted. After all, these researchers were implying that police officials could not be trusted to administer fair lineups; that we (the police) were cheating, lying and then committing perjury in court to cover up these misdeeds.

We had previously reviewed the research material provided before our meeting, but hearing this type of statement spoken out loud was an attack on our professionalism, it was hard not to take it personally. The only two circumstances saving the entire project at this point turned out to be that it was proposed in a non-threatening manner (it was also pointed out that every clinical study is conducted double blind to prevent favoritism in the results) and it was the end of the day and the law enforcement members would have the evening and night to think about the statement.

By the next morning, we were aware of three important facts. First, the researchers had tried to make it clear that utilizing a double blind procedure was in no way meant to imply that purposeful deception was being employed by law enforcement. Second, the premise of witness bolstering was a new circumstance that needed to be further examined. Thirdly, Sgt. Carroll remembered that, in many cases, a double blind procedure was already in effect, if not written into a formal procedure.

To more fully explain our thinking, after reflection, it seemed to us that the identification administrator might unknowingly make some gesture or comment that might influence the witness. After all, we remember being excited that we may finally be removing a vicious predator from society. Also, the witness may expect some help from the detective knowing that the detective wouldn't let them pick the wrong person from the lineup.

The idea and results of witness bolstering were relatively unknown to us. After careful review of some of the studies behind this concept, we believe that this bolstering occurs on more occasions than not and severely affect the witness's certainty level. Double blind identification procedures effectively eliminate this problem.

In one study, a group of people were shown a shaky video of an alleged crime in progress. These witnesses were then shown a lineup which did contain the actual offender. One half of those witnesses viewing the video and identifying a suspect weren't given any feedback regarding their choice. The other half was informed, after their identifications of a suspect, that they had identified the right person. The witnesses were then administered a questionnaire concerning the lineup. The group that received no feedback reported that 12% were certain of their identifications, 4% reported having a good look at the suspect (which is good in that they weren't provided a good look), 3% reported getting a good look at the suspect's face (also a good result because they did not receive a good look at the suspect's face).

Results from the group that was informed that they had identified the suspect revealed that 44% were sure of their identifications, 27% reported that they had a good look at the suspect and finally, 19% reported getting a good look at the suspect's face.

In other words, just the innocuous or innocent statement by the lineup administrator of "you picked the right guy" altered witnesses' memory.

Finally, after careful consideration, Sgt. Carroll remembered that during his career in the detective division on many occasions the unit desk officer would administer photo lineups. Sgt. Carroll had a routine where he would set aside a couple of hours each week for the purpose of conducting photo lineups (he and his partner were assigned about thirty-five to forty robbery cases a month). Victims and witnesses would be contacted and asked to come into the detective office on a specified day where they were shown some form of photo identification procedure. If a real suspect had been developed, a group of loose photos were obtained and a lineup would be conducted. On occasion, a major case investigation would come in and Sgt. Carroll was often unable to personally conduct the identification procedure. On those occasions, the unit desk officer would be given the photos in an envelope identified with the victim's name and case number. When the witness arrived, s/he would be shown the lineup and the results would be documented on the envelope. The victim was contacted sometime later to confirm the procedure and a report documenting the procedure would be prepared and submitted.

So it seems that after all the heartache concerning double blind identification procedures, it appeared that we were already using the technique.

The only drawback we have found is that a double blind procedure requires the officer conducting the identification procedure to prepare the lineup report, taking time from his/her duties. That fact alone may require the lineup administrator to appear in court. However, we have found in practical experience that the lineup officer is rarely subpoenaed to court. After all, his/her entire testimony is on the supplemental report and s/he has no additional information about the case. The same information can be solicited from the witness when s/he testifies.

When we propose double blind procedures during our training classes, the comments range from "what are you crazy?" to "I have a rapport with the victim, that's important to the case solution." The comments are always the same, law enforcement personnel must somehow think the same, "It'll cost the department overtime money for court appearances, and we can't do that." Our response has also been the same, review the literature try it and then decide. We have found the opposite occurs. Double blind procedures, combined with sequential procedures effectively remove the basis for defense attorney's motions to suppress the identification.

Chapter 12
Live ID Procedures

Millions of television and motion picture viewers are familiar with the stereotype police lineup where a group of suspects are either up on a stage or in a room and a witness is then brought into the room or an adjoining room and attempts to make an identification. While this type of identification procedure has great dramatic value, it would appear that most law enforcement agencies throughout the country rely almost exclusively on photographic or digital images for identification purposes as evidence.

Our experience and limited research reveals that it is mainly the larger law enforcement agencies throughout the country that rely on live identifications to formally charge a suspect with a crime. The smaller law enforcement departments rely almost exclusively on photographs for identification and formal charging of offenders.

According to the U.S. Department of Justice, Bureau of Justice Statistics, almost 86% of local, county and state law enforcement agencies employ less than 100 sworn personnel each.[64] It is the larger law enforcement agencies (14% of the total law enforcement agencies) that conduct identification procedures more frequently, due mainly to the amount of crime occurring in their jurisdictions. These agencies, along with the volume of crime handled, also are

---

[64] *Census of State and Law Enforcement Local Enforcement Agencies,* 2008, U.S. Department of Justice, Office of Justice Programs, Bureau of Justice Statistics, NCJ 233982, July 2011.

required to conduct the greatest number of identification procedures.

We firmly believe that live identification procedures are superior to digital image or photographic identification procedures. For those readers who have conducted both types of identification procedures some of the reasons for this preference are obvious. Other reasons are not so obvious to those who have not conducted live procedures.

As we have stated earlier, one of the reasons that we believe in the use of show-ups (within the judicial guidelines established) rests on the facts that a show-up is both timely and the suspect is presented live. This affords the witness an opportunity to view the suspect, his height, clothing and mannerisms immediately following the crime. A show-up also allows for the timely recovery of corroborating evidence. If an identification is obtained and probable cause to arrest the suspect is established, the search incident to the arrest will usually lead to the recovery of weapons, currency and identifiable property.

In jurisdictions that use photographic or digital images for the limited purpose to obtain probable cause to arrest, the law enforcement agencies follow the preference set forth by the courts in states like Illinois.

Courtesy of Cook County District Attorney's Office, Illinois

The Illinois courts prefer live lineup identifications over photographic methods when a suspect is in custody and a live lineup is therefore possible.[65] The Illinois courts have repeatedly stated if a live line-up is feasible (like when a suspect is in custody on another charge) a photographic identification should not be done. In the Commonwealth of Massachusetts however, a suspect may not be forced to stand in a live identification procedure absent probable cause.[66]

Contrary to the thinking of the Illinois courts, the Massachusetts courts have ruled that even if a live lineup could be arranged, the police may resort to using a photo array.[67] The challenge to law enforcement then is to obtain admissible evidence of probable cause to arrest and charge an individual. Consider where a suspect happens to be in custody for a crime and he is suspected in additional, unrelated cases. To satisfy the court's preference for live identification procedures (at least in Illinois), the preferred identification procedure would be a live lineup. A live lineup would be scheduled and the suspect would be placed in that lineup. This procedure may require the assistance of the County Sheriff's Office if the suspect is in their custody and the investigating agency is a local or state police department. If the working relationship between the sheriff and the local agency is good, it may be possible to conduct a live lineup at the county jail. Sometimes (depending on precedent, custom or law), it may be necessary to obtain a court order to either conduct the identification procedure itself or to temporarily transfer custody of the suspect from the sheriff to the investigating law enforcement

---

[65] See *People v. Holiday*, 47 Ill. 2nd 300, 307, 265 N.E. 2nd 634 (1970) and *People v. Kubat*, 94 Ill. 2d 437, 60 Ill. Dec 30, 447, N.E. 2d 247

[66] *Commonwealth v Holland*, 410 Mass. 248 (1991) and *Commonwealth v Bumpus* 362 Mass. 672 (1972)

[67] *Comm. V. Gerrior*, 13 Mass. App. Ct. 913 (1982)

agency. After all of this work, conducting a lineup with the suspect now becomes only a problem of scheduling and logistics.[68]

What if an investigation points to a suspect and s/he is not in custody on another charge? The question now becomes how do I develop probable cause? The obvious answer is to obtain a preliminary identification with a photographic/image lineup. If I obtain a positive identification from a victim, why couldn't the suspect be charged with the additional crime? Remember that in some jurisdictions, the preferred identification of a suspect is in a live lineup. If there are multiple victims/witnesses, this becomes less of a problem. After receiving one photo identification from a witness, the rest of the witnesses are held for a live lineup. These additional victims or witnesses would not be allowed to view the photographic/digital procedure.

According to researchers, however, it is redundant to have a live lineup procedure after a victim/witness has already made an identification from a photo or digital image. The researchers refer to this procedure as a confirmation. The researchers also state" who would you expect the witness to pick; after all he has already identified a suspect."[69] Others are convinced that common sense tells you the witness will pick out the person he has already identified. When researchers are confronted as to why they believe

---

[68] Some court cases have ruled that even without probable cause, a suspect in custody for an unrelated crime may be compelled to participate in a lineup. See *U.S. v. Anderson*, 490 F. 2d 785 (D.C. Cir 1974), *Adams v. U.S.* 399 F 2d 574 (D.C. Cir 1968), *People v. Hall*, 242 N.W. 2nd 377 (Mich 1976) and *Pedgeon v. Rubin*, 435 N.Y.U.S. 2nd 763 (N.Y. 1981)

[69] Conversation with Professor Nancy Steblay, October 2, 2009 at Columbus, Ohio airport.

this outcome is the most probable result, they have on occasion answered the data tends to indicate[70] that this will occur.[71]

We have not found much research concerning the confirmation identification procedure.[72] This may be because the researchers publish the results of their work in professional journals for peer review and comment, not publications normally reviewed by criminal justice practitioners. It is also possible that research on the confirmation identification is limited because studies with live subjects are extremely expensive and difficult to conduct.[73]

We (more so Sgt. Carroll who is more familiar with and has conducted hundreds of live lineup procedures) rely on their combined years of experience conducting lineups and confirmation identification procedures. On many occasions victims or witnesses who have tentatively identified a suspect in a photographic lineup come to view a live lineup and state "Number 3 is the guy whose photo I picked, but, he is not the man that robbed me." It is at these times that we hear responses like this that we are gratified that additional identification steps were taken. Remember that people change from the time that their photographs were taken or the color of the photo may be off. The confirmation lineup identification procedure allows the witness to view the suspect's mannerisms in more detail.

The need to obtain probable cause will forever be the catalyst to use photos and digital images to acquire that probable cause. We will admit here that guesses and hunches should never be used

---

[70] We possess great respect and admiration for the researchers, are excited by and believe in their efforts. However, every time we hear "The data tends to indicate" from the researchers we think that this is shorthand for we haven't studied that and really don't know.

[71] Conversation with Professor Gary Wells, mid September 2000, Baltimore Co., Maryland Police Academy

[72] The only exception is the discredited Chicago, Illinois Study Available at www.chicagopolice.org/IL%20Pilot%20on%20Eyewitness%20ID.pdf

[73] Conversation with Professor Jennifer Dysart, April 12, 2011 at the Police Executive Research Forum (PERF),Technical Assistance Group (TAG) Meeting, Crystal City Marriott Hotel, Washington, DC.

solely to come up with a suspect. Before anyone's image being placed in an identification procedure there must be something other than a hunch or feeling. We also want to remind the reader, whenever possible; evidence along with an identification should be obtained before any charges being filed. We have become aware of cases where officers have obtained an arrest warrant for a deceased suspect after obtaining a photographic identification. Complete, thorough investigations are the standard sought in every criminal case. The reader is reminded that the photo identification of a suspect is only one part of the investigation. Corroboration should always be sought.

We want to stress that: 1) If probable cause exists before a photo lineup is conducted, the suspect should be arrested first and then shown only in a live lineup. 2) If there are multiple victims and/or witnesses, once one photo identification has been obtained, the additional witnesses should view a live lineup and should never see the photographic procedure. According to many courts, this type of procedure may strengthen a witness's photographic identification. The courts take note of the fact that some victims or witnesses are reluctant to positively identify a suspect without personally observing the suspect in person.[74] 3) Because the photo identification is used only for probable cause to arrest, the witness does not need to make a positive identification. The suspect will not be charged based solely on the photo id. Additional investigation will need to be conducted and a live lineup identification obtained before formal charges are brought. 4) It may be weeks or months (sometimes over a year) between the photo identification and the suspect's arrest. We hear objections to the confirmation identification from those who think that the police get a photo identification and immediately put the suspect in a live identification procedure. That should never occur.

The benefits of live procedures are many. We want to point out some of those benefits:

---

[74] See *Commonwealth v. Levasseur*, 32 Mass. App. Ct, 629 (1992)

1). **The identification by the victim or witness may be more reliable.** We have found that when witnesses see suspects in person, they tend to be surer of their identifications and are more likely to dismiss or disregard the innocent suspect.

2). **When a suspect is arrested it takes time to prepare a live lineup.** Fillers or shills must be found. These fillers must be similar in description to the suspect. In larger agencies, suitable arrested persons may be available in their custody in their detention facility. (Experience has suggested, at least, that if your suspect is a white male, no white males fitting his description are in custody. The same usually applies if your suspect is a female, etc. Consider also that your suspect may have pink or green hair or a tattoo on his face). Some law enforcement agencies may be able to use the facilities and arrested subjects at the county jail. If no matching fillers are immediately available in law enforcement's custody, volunteers must be located and transported to the lineup location. Law enforcement personnel should only be used as fillers in identification procedures as a last resort.

3). **The time needed to prepare the live lineup can be used to great benefit of the investigation.** A suspect left alone in an interview room has time for his mind to work. Many suspects have been known to feel remorse when alone with their thoughts. The suspect may exhibit guilty tendencies. According to author David Simon, rule number 4, in his ten rules of homicide investigation, contained in his book *Homicide, a Year on the Killing Streets,* a guilty man left alone in an interview room will go to sleep.[75] Experience has shown us that innocent suspects tend to pace the interview room like a caged tiger. Observation of these tendencies and the suspect's conscience may lead to a confession that may not have been forthcoming had you just arrested and charged the subject.

4). **The suspect may confess in the presence of your fillers.** When the fillers have been assembled, take the suspect to the

---

[75] David Simon *Homicide, a Year on the Killing Streets,* , Houghton, Mifflin 8 1991 & 2006

lineup location and place him with those fillers. Explain to the suspect that he has a choice of the position he will be shown in and ask him if he understands the procedure. Leave the suspect with the fillers along with a detective. It is possible that the fillers and the suspect will begin conversing about why they are all present at the lineup. Very often your suspect will make an incriminating statement.

5). **During the live lineup the suspect may make an incriminating statement.** We have had experiences where during a live identification procedure the suspect makes a statement. On one of Sgt. Carroll's cases a suspect was being viewed through a one way glass (the glass is not completely one way) said, "I remember her, I robbed her twice last week."

6). **Consider a voice identification procedure if the suspect was masked or spoke extensively during the crime.** Although the need for voice identifications is not as necessary as physical identifications, the use of this procedure should not be overlooked. Several points need to be remembered, however, when considering a voice lineup. It is common practice (on television at least) that when a voice identification is conducted, the lineup participants repeat the words spoken by the perpetrator during the crime. Some jurisdictions restrict, discourage or forbid this practice.[76] In our experience, it has been beneficial to conduct a voice identification after a physical lineup. Before the voice identification, the order of the participants should be shuffled to ensure that the suspect is in a different spot than he was for the live identification. It is hard to defend two identifications of the same individual (one live and one voice) when the suspect was in the number three spot for a live identification and number five for a voice identification. It is essential that voice identifications be conducted in a manner so the victim or witness cannot see the person speaking.[77]

---

[76] See *Commonwealth v. Miles*, 420 Mass. 67 (1995) and Commonwealth v. Marini, 375 Mass. 510 (1978)

[77] See *Commonwealth v. DeMaria*, 46 Mass. App. Ct. 114 (1999)

Masked defendants have been convicted after having been tentatively identified by their body shape in a live lineup and then their voice identified. Consider also that if a suspect has been voice identified, he may be more likely to confess and lead the investigator to additional corroborative evidence.

7). **The time after the live lineup can be used to gather further evidence.** After a live lineup identification, a suspect is more likely to confess because he knows that he has been picked out.

A suspect may also wish to apologize to his victim. Some courts have ruled that only a guilty person would offer an apology to a victim. However, this apology must contain more than just 'I'm sorry." To be admitted in court as an admission of guilt, the suspect must convey what he is sorry for. Therefore, a statement such as "I'm sorry that I hurt you when I took your purse" would be much more compelling.[78] Another benefit of an apology to the victim is that the perpetrator has now reverse identified the victim. This can be especially helpful in cases where the victim was less than positive regarding their lineup identification.

After a lineup identification we recommend that a suspect's ID photos (direct and both profiles) be taken along with those photographs taken to document the participants of the identification procedure. When the suspect's id photos are taken, be sure that the suspect is standing next to the posted rights card in the interview or squad room. These photos will assist the prosecutor if a motion to suppress the suspect's statement is filed. Most motions to suppress statements begin by stating that the suspect was never given his rights.

The longer the investigator has lawful personal custody of the suspect, the more likely it is that additional corroborative evidence will be obtained. This ensures that the actual offender is charged and subsequently convicted of the crime.

---

[78] See *Usher v. Jones*, 943 F.2nd 889 (8th Circuit 1991), *U.S. v. Lutz*, 621 F. 2nd 940 (9th Circuit 1980), *Pieczynski v. Florida*, 516 So. 2nd 1048 (Fl. 1987), *McKim v. Indiana*, 476 NE 2d 503 (Indiana 1985).

Chapter 13
Operational Procedures for Eyewitness Identification of Suspects

When interviewing the victim or witness of any crime (either by the preliminary or follow up investigator), remember that most of the time s/he is frightened, nervous and upset. I think we can all agree that quite a few of these victims and witnesses wish they had been somewhere other than where the crime occurred. In our experiences, we have found it normal for a victim or witness when asked to describe the suspect, to do a fair job. When that witness or victim is asked if s/he would be able to identify the offender, a common response is that s/he does not think that they would be able to recognize the person later. The victim/witness then relates how nervous they are.

In our experience, most of these witnesses are able to identify the suspect in a lineup later. We recommend that the investigator gently press the witness to soften their response and not be rigid in their answer. Once a statement from the victim or witness that s/he cannot identify the offender is memorialized in a police report, the statement may be used by the defense attorney to impeach the victim/witness at a trial.

It is not necessary for an attorney to be present at a photographic or live lineup prior to an indictment or formal charge situations. We believe that this places a greater responsibility on the criminal investigator to be aware of the rights of our citizens. If these rights are violated, the courts may require additional safeguards during identification procedures in the future.

Fair composition of an identification procedure enables the witness to provide a more accurate identification or non-identification. The investigator should compose the lineup in such a manner that the suspect does not unduly stand out. In composing a lineup, the investigator should include only one suspect in each identification procedure. The problem with multiple suspect lineups is that the probability of a possible mistaken identification increases dramatically as the number of suspects in a lineup increases. If more than one suspect must be shown in any one lineup, the fillers must be multiplied accordingly (e.g., two suspects would require a minimum of ten fillers, for total of twelve participants).

Select fillers who generally fit the witness's description of the perpetrator. When there is a limited/inadequate description of the perpetrator provided by the witness, or when the description of the perpetrator differs significantly from the appearance of the suspect, fillers should resemble the suspect in significant features. This does not mean that the fillers must closely resemble the suspect (see notes under procedure 5 below). If the description does not fit the suspect on some characteristic (e.g., the witness described dark hair, yet the suspect has light hair), then the fillers should match the suspect on that characteristic rather than matching the description on that characteristic. Consider that complete uniformity of features is not required or desirable. The standard to apply here is that the suspect should not unduly stand out.

If multiple photos of the suspect are reasonably available to the investigator, select a photo that resembles the suspect's description or appearance at the time of the incident. The most recent photo of the suspect is not necessarily the best one to use if the suspect's appearance has changed since the time of the crime. For example, the suspect may intentionally change his or her appearance.

Include a minimum of five fillers (non-suspects) per photo or digital image identification procedure; a minimum of four fillers is suggested for live lineup procedures. These are suggested minimum numbers; some jurisdictions might require more fillers, others less. Consider that complete uniformity of features is neither required nor desirable. Avoid using fillers that so closely resemble the suspect that a person familiar with the suspect might find it difficult to distinguish the suspect from the fillers. In their efforts to ensure that the suspect's photo does not unduly stand out, police have often gone to great lengths to ensure that all members of a lineup look as similar to one another as possible, including the suspect.

Courtesy of ADA Winn Collins, Dane County, Wisconsin

Making the fillers closely resemble the suspect is not advised because a lineup in which all the people look very similar to one another actually reduces the chances of an accurate identification by a witness and increases the chances that a filler would be picked out in error.

Consider creating a consistent appearance between the suspect and fillers with respect to any unique or unusual feature (e.g., scars or tattoos) used to describe the perpetrator by artificially adding or concealing that feature. If there is a unique feature/characteristic described by the witness, such as a scar, the preferred procedure is to leave the unique feature visible and select fillers with a similar feature/characteristic. Sometimes police may choose to enhance the fillers with a similar feature (still ensuring that the suspect does not unduly stand out). If the suspect has a unique feature not described by the witness, you should not alter the suspect's photo. Rather you should select fillers that have similar, but not identical, feature or enhance the fillers with a similar feature.

Consider placing the suspect in different positions in each lineup if he is a suspect in multiple crimes or with multiple witnesses in the same case. Position the suspect randomly in the lineup or, in live lineups you may want to consider allowing the suspect (or his attorney) to choose his position. Some witnesses can be reserved for later identification procedures. This ensures different identification procedures, validates the results of earlier identification procedures and may reduce defense motions concerning witnesses conferring regarding which subject to pick. When showing a new suspect, avoid reusing fillers in lineups shown to the same witness.

Ensure that no writings or information concerning previous arrest(s) will be visible to the witness. Some witnesses might try to extract meaning from any arrest dates or other markings on the photos. Such information could lead some witnesses to make faulty inferences. Booking plates, for instance, can be covered with tape or removed from the image. Also ensure that no writings indicating previous witnesses' identifications are visible to the witness.

To ensure that the suspect does not unduly stand out, consider showing the lineup to people unfamiliar with the case and ask them if they can identify the suspect. In general, if the lineup is properly constructed, a person who is given the verbal description of the perpetrator (as described by the witness) should not be able to tell which person is the suspect in the case.

Recite the identification procedure instructions and ask the witness if they understand the procedure. Some departments may want the administrator to sign the instruction form as a way to prove the instructions were presented. Other departments prefer that the witness sign the form, while still other departments require both the witness and the administrator to sign the form, attesting to the fact that the witness read and understood the instructions and was witnessed by the administrator.

We feel that the subsequently prepared supplemental report detailing the facts that the instructions were read to the witness, the witness identified or failed to identify anyone coupled with that administrator's sworn testimony in a court of law, are sufficient to prove the facts presented. However, we will yield to local policy or custom.

Present each photo or image to the witness separately, in a previously determined order, removing those previously shown. Let the witness determine when to view the next photo. There should never be more than one photograph or image displayed at a time.

Avoid saying anything to the witness that may influence the witness's selection. Ideally, nothing should be said to the witness because it might indicate which person the investigator believes is the perpetrator or that the investigator believes that the perpetrator is definitely in the lineup. Also, anything said to the witness might interfere with his/her ability to concentrate on the task. If something needs to be said to facilitate the procedure, it should not convey any information about the identity of the suspect (e.g., NOT "I noticed you pointed at number two," BUT rather, "would it help for me to explain the instructions again?") Following this procedure is especially important with the sequential lineup because only one photo is being viewed at any given time.

If an identification is made, avoid reporting to the witness any information regarding the individual s/he has selected prior to obtaining any witness's statement of certainty. If the investigator wants to question the witness about certainty, the witness should not be told anything about the status of the person identified at this point (e.g., do not say, that is the person we have as a suspect, or that is the same person that another witness picked; do not say anything that discounts the witness's selection, such as, that person is not a suspect.) This includes nonverbal reactions, such as facial expressions.

You must show all the images/individuals and listen carefully to any comments made by the witness when and if an identification is made. An investigator must be careful not to questioning a certainty statement at this point as it could inadvertently redirect the witness or question their judgment.

Record any identification results and witness's statement of certainty. Document in writing the photo lineup procedures, including identification information and sources of all photos used, names of all persons present at the photo lineup and date and time of the identification procedure. Advise the witness not to discuss the identification procedure or its results with other witnesses involved in the case and discourage contact with the media. Remind the witness that discussing the results of the procedure could harm the investigation.

Preserve the presentation order of the lineup. In addition, the photos themselves should be preserved in their original condition. To defend legal challenges to the lineup procedures, it is critical to reproduce the original lineup for presentation in future proceedings. It is advisable to retain the original photos as evidence or, alternatively, photocopy (in color if possible) the original lineup to produce a copy in the event that one or more of the original photographs cannot be reproduced and to preserve an accurate representation of the order of the photos.

When preparing your lineup, consider that your witness should not be aware of the number of images, photographs or persons s/he will be asked to view. This is not suggested to confuse the witness, instead it is meant to alleviate the nervousness a witness may develop as the number of possibilities from which to make a selection diminishes.

With photos or images, the pile will never get smaller if after viewing each one it is placed on the bottom. You may find it easier to put each image or photograph in a folder before showing them to the witness. In this case the investigator may wish to add some empty folders to the pile. The possibilities are limited only by the creativeness of the lineup administrator.

Additional viewing (laps) of the same lineup is not recommended by the research community. Additional viewing dilutes the benefits of the sequential procedure and provides the witness a way to employ a modified form of relative judgment. However, in keeping with our preference for the identification procedure to be somewhat user friendly, in those cases where it is deemed advisable or necessary to re-show the lineup, we recommend that the images or photographs be shuffled so they are not presented in the same order as the previous showing. Be aware that the procedure must be reported accurately and a second lap through the procedure may diminish the value of the identification. Research from Hennepin County (Minneapolis) Minnesota reveals that accurate identifications drop dramatically after the first viewing with a corresponding increase in filler picks.

For live presentations the administrator must keep the subjects out of sight and present them one at a time. This procedure is not nearly as cumbersome as is sounds.

As we have previously discussed, the lineup administrator must then prepare and submit the supplemental report concerning the procedure.

Special Circumstances: Juvenile victims/witnesses

Juvenile witnesses create special problems for the investigator. Here, we comment only on having the results of an identification procedure admitted in court. One of the techniques we have been successful with for younger witnesses is the use of multiple identification procedures. The prosecution must be able to show the judge that the juvenile witness understands the difference between the truth and a lie and must also show that the juvenile didn't just happen to identify the suspect. First, the lineup administrator must prepare three different sets of fillers, either live or photo. The first lineup is conducted with a photo (or a person) that the young witness knows, like a neighbor. This photo or persons replaces the suspect in the procedure. The second lineup is conducted with all strangers.   The third lineup is then conducted with the actual suspect present.

If all goes according to plan, after viewing the first procedure, the juvenile witness will identify the person he knows. Then, after viewing the second procedure, the witness correctly states that no one s/he recognizes was in that lineup.   The investigator/ administrator can then be confident when, after the third lineup, the young witness identifies the suspect.   As with all special circumstance cases, check with the prosecutor's office or the department legal advisor before administering this type identification procedure.

Special Circumstances: Live ID procedures

It is well established that a suspect's right to counsel attaches after significant judicial proceedings have begun, i.e.; formal charge, preliminary hearing, indictment, arraignment or information.[79] It is suggested that if this right exists in the case you are investigating, the suspect should be advised that s/he is entitled to an attorney.   No such constitutional guarantee is afforded a suspect who has not been previously charged or indicted. While this reflects the law of the land, we believe that any defense attorney who attends an identification procedure is doing his/her client a disservice.

When a defense attorney appears at a law enforcement facility, he is out of his element. As opposed to what is seen on television shows, like *Law and Order*, attorneys are not free to roam around the facility. You will never see a defense lawyer walk in on an interrogation or live id procedure and stop the proceedings. When a defense attorney attends a live lineup procedure, he/she is a spectator or witness, not an active participant in the proceedings. The defense attorney is not entitled to make any comments, intimidate the witnesses or disrupt the procedure. If the lawyer inserts himself into the proceedings or interferes with the orderly

---

[79] *U.S. v Wade*, 388, US 218, *Moore v. Illinois* 434 U.S. 220 (1977), *Commonwealth v. Simmonds*, 386 Mass. 234, 1982.

identification process, he can be escorted from the facility. The reader is reminded that in criminal cases, the suspect/defendant has constitutional rights, not the attorney. It is important to remember that any constitutional right a suspect has may also be intelligently waived. Just because the suspect has a right to an attorney, it doesn't mean that a lawyer must be present if the suspect doesn't want a lawyer.

If an attorney arrives and wishes to view the identification procedure, it has been the practice of the authors to allow the lawyer access even if the suspect's constitutional right to an attorney has not yet attached. The authors allow the defense lawyer to assist with the selection of fillers and the position where the suspect (his client) will be viewed. (Ensure that these facts are reported in the lineup supplemental report prepared after the procedure.) The reason for allowing the attorney to participant is simple. Later, the defense attorney becomes, in essence, a witness for the prosecution. It is extremely difficult to file a motion to suppress a pretrial identification if the lawyer helped assemble the participants. This places a greater burden on the lineup administrator to ensure that the lineup is fair.

One of the most common tactics is for the defense attorney to send an investigator to view the procedure. It should be noted here that there is no constitutional right to a defense investigator at any time. Defense investigators have no standing to observe the lineup. Some attorneys have been known to attempt to disrupt the proceedings to deliberately get removed from the premises. Then the attorney files a motion to suppress the identification in court due lack of legal representation. The lineup administrator must thoroughly document the attorney's actions.

Another defense tactic is to attempt to delay the lineup stating that his schedule is tight or that the police should conduct the identification procedure at a better time (business hours instead of 9:00 P.M.). The live lineup procedure should be scheduled when it is convenient for the victim, witnesses and the lineup administrator.[80]

While conducting training seminars around the country, defense attorneys have stated to us that if I knew the police were using double blind procedures and the witnesses and victim were given instructions, I would not feel the need to attend the live identification procedure.

Recording Identification Results

The record of the outcome of the identification procedure accurately and completely reflects the identification results obtained from the witness. When conducting an identification procedure, the investigator should preserve the outcome of the procedure by documenting any identification or non-identification results obtained from the witness. When conducting an identification procedure, the investigator should record both identification and non-identification results in writing, including the witness's own words regarding how sure s/he is, ensure results are signed and dated by the witness, ensure that no materials indicating previous identification results are visible to the witness, and ensure that the witness does not write on or mark any materials that will be used in other identification procedures. In jurisdictions where it is required that a witness signs the back of a selected photo; ensure that the signed photo is not used in a later identification procedure.

Reports regarding show ups, driving the victim/witness around the area in an attempt to identify a suspect or suspect vehicle or attempts to identify recovered property, can simply state what occurred and the result in narrative form.

---

[80] In some jurisdictions it may be required for a suspect to waive his right to an attorney at a live lineup or the lineup must be conducted when the attorney can attend. See *Commonwealth v. Torres*, 442 Mass. 554 (2004). It is suggested that lineup administrators check their prosecutor and/or their department legal advisor.

The report should be prepared and submitted by the person conducting the procedure, not the case officer if the procedure was conducted by a blind administrator.

A complete and accurate record of the details and outcome of the identification procedure can be a critical document in the investigation and any subsequent legal proceedings. As such, the report should be prepared immediately at the conclusion of the identification procedure.

ANY time ANY identification procedure is conducted, a report must be prepared and submitted. The procedure may be included in the narrative of the original case report during the preliminary investigation if the procedure occurs immediately after the incident. This holds equally true for negative procedures (where no one is selected), negative show ups (one on one procedures), and driving the victim around the area looking for suspects or viewing automobiles.

Every live lineup that results in an identification also REQUIRES digital, photographic or video documentation along with the required supplementary report.

Note: When testifying in court regarding the visual documentation of the identification procedure, the best answer is usually "the photograph speaks for itself." The defense has been educated to the fact that for appeal purposes most times the justices reviewing the case have only the written transcript to rely on. When the defense attorney phrases a closed ended question (a question that limits the response) such as, "Isn't it true detective, that my client is the only person in this lineup wearing a white shirt?" he is attempting to make it seem like his client unduly stands out among all the participants. It may be true that the defendant is the only subject in the photograph wearing a white shirt, but every lineup member is wearing a different color shirt. Therefore, the defendant does not unduly stand out among the participants. This example may be problematic if the offender was originally described as having worn a white shirt. Investigators must be aware that lineup participants can be attired all in the same clothes or all different clothes. However, this needs to be addressed at the time of the identification procedure. your response is the photograph speaks for itself, the appellate court will probably refer to visual documentation and not rely on just the written transcript.

Chapter 14
Forms & Procedural Orders

A report is required any time an identification procedure is conducted. The report should include, but is not limited to, the following information:

DATE, TIME & LOCATION
OF PROCEDURE: Self Explanatory

PERSONS CONDUCTING LINEUP: Rank, Name, Badge#, Unit. State if A Blind Administrator

PERSONS PRESENT AT LINEUP: Attorneys, Lock Up Keepers, Arresting Officers, Supervisors, (anyone except those conducting).

PERSONS VIEWING LINEUP: 1-Victim(s) (time viewed)
                               2-Witness(es) (time viewed)

PERSONS PORTRAYED IN   (list from left to right)
LINEUP: 1-LAST NAME, FIRST NAME, SEX, RACE, DOB, HEIGHT, WEIGHT, ARREST (Jail), SID, FBI NUMBER.
                               2-through end-repeat info

PERSON IDENTIFIED: List by Name, Image, Folder or Photo number.

VIEWER CERTAINTY STATEMENT: The exact words stated by victim/witness positive or negative.

HISTORY & INVESTIGATION: This section should contain what procedures were employed; simultaneous, sequential, double blind sequential or loose photos/images. It should fully describe the specifics of the procedure employed, one image in each of six folders, shown one at time after being shuffled, etc. The report should also state clearly that the administrator has no knowledge of the incident, if that is the case.

This report should be prepared and submitted by the person conducting the procedure, not the case officer if the procedure was conducted by a blind administrator.

Reports regarding show ups, driving the victim/witness around the area in an attempt to identify a suspect or suspect vehicle, or attempts to identify recovered property, can simply state what occurred and the result in narrative form.

Show-Up Instructions

1-I am going to take you to view a person.

2-Please do not infer anything because he is with the police.

3-This person is not under arrest and has not been charged with any crime.

4-This person may or may not be the person that you observed committing the crime.

5-It is just as important to clear innocent persons as it is to identify the guilty person.

6-If you identify this person as the one who committed the crime, procedure requires that I ask you to state, in your own words, how certain you are of your identification.

7-If you do not identify this person; we will continue to investigate your case.

8-Do you have any questions?

Lineup Instructions

1-I am going to show you a group of photographs/images/individuals.

2-The photographs/images/individuals are in a random order.

3-These photographs/images/individuals will be viewed one at a time.

4-Take as much time as you need to make a decision about each one before moving to the next.

5-The person who committed the crime may or may not be in the lineup.

6-It is just as important to clear innocent persons from suspicion as it is to identify the guilty person.

7-Individuals in the lineup may not appear exactly as they did at the time of the incident.[81]

8-If you do not make an identification the police will continue to investigate the case.

9-If you make an identification, procedure requires that you indicate in your own words how certain you are of the identification.

10-All photographs/images/persons will be shown even if an identification is obtained earlier.

11-I have no additional information concerning this investigation.

12-Do not indicate to any other witness that you have or have not made an identification.

---

[81] see previous discussion regarding this instruction

The following pages illustrate a Sequential Blind Administration policy that is being utilized in totality or various forms in police department's across the country.

EYEWITNESS IDENTIFICATION PROCEDURE

Table of Contents

INTRODUCTORY DISCUSSION

GENERAL GUIDELINES

TYPE OF EYEWITNESS EVIDENCE PROCEDURES

OTHER METHODS OF IDENTIFICATION

DOCUMENTING RESULTS OF IDENTIFICATION

I. Introductory Discussion:

A. Nowhere more so than in criminal cases does the legal system rely on the testimony of eyewitnesses. The evidence eyewitnesses provide can be tremendously helpful in developing leads, identifying criminals, and exonerating the innocent.

Therefore, the XYZ Police Department has established the following policies/procedures with regard to the collection and handling of eyewitness evidence.

The intent of this policy is to:
Combine research and practical perspectives;
Promote accuracy in eyewitness evidence and;
Promote sound professional practices.

II. General Guidelines & Types of Eyewitness Evidence

A. **Lineups:** A display of photos or persons consisting of one
           suspect
among a number of fillers from which a witness can identify a
perpetrator. Lineups will be composed in such a manner that the
suspect does not unduly stand out. Lineups shall be presented in
the sequential fashion as described.

Sequential Photo/Live Lineup: Photographs or individuals are
viewed by the witness one at a time in random order.

Note: Live lineup presentation order may be determined by the
investigator and consideration given to the suspect's and/or their
attorney's request for a certain position within the lineup.

Double Blind Procedures: Double blind testing means that the
person administering the lineup (Independent Administrator) does
not know the desired answer (the suspect). Utilizing this practice,
the Independent Administrator would not be aware of which
member of the photo spread or lineup is the suspect and would
eliminate the possibility of influencing the witness' selection.

B. **Digital Imaging System:** Digital Imaging Systems are
           collections
of photos of previously arrested persons which may be used in
cases where a suspect has or has not yet been determined and other
reliable sources have been exhausted. Showing witnesses images
from this system may provide a possible suspect, but the results
should be evaluated with extreme caution.

C. **Composites:** A composite is a sketch (computer generated or
artist) based on the witness's descriptive information that enable
officers and citizens to better perceive how a suspect may appear.
Composite images can be beneficial investigative tools; however,

they should not be used as stand-alone evidence and ***DO NOT, by themselves,*** rise to the level of probable cause.

D. **Show-ups:** A show-up is a field identification procedure performed when circumstances require the prompt display of a single suspect to a single victim or witness. The inherent suggestiveness of the encounter can be minimized through the use of procedural safeguards.

III. Procedures

A. **Composing Lineups:** The identification procedure should be conducted in a manner that promotes the accuracy, reliability, fairness and objectivity of the witness' identification. The following procedures will result in the composition of a lineup in which a suspect does not unduly stand out.

1. Photo Lineups: When presenting a photo lineup, lineup administrator will:

a. Include only one suspect in each identification procedure.

b. Select fillers (non-suspects) who generally fit the witness's description of the perpetrator. When there is a limited or inadequate description of the perpetrator provided by the witness, or when the description of the perpetrator differs significantly from the appearance of the suspect, fillers should resemble the suspect in significant features.

c. Select a photo that resembles the suspect's description or appearance at the time of the incident if multiple photos of the suspect are reasonably available to the investigator.

d. Include a minimum of five fillers (non-suspect) per identification procedure. Once the photos are selected, the investigator/administrator shall mark the back of each photo with numbers and record the order in which they were shown on the form provided.

e. Consider that complete uniformity of features is neither required or desirable. Avoid using fillers who so closely resemble the suspect that a person familiar with the suspect might find it difficult to distinguish the suspect from the fillers.

f. Create a consistent appearance between the suspect and fillers with respect to any unique feature (e.g., scars, tattoos) used to describe the perpetrator by using images that cover these characteristics.

g. Position the suspect randomly in each lineup, both across multiple cases and cases with multiple witnesses.

h. When showing a new suspect, avoid reusing fillers in lineups shown to the same witness.

i. Ensure that no writings or information concerning previous arrest (s) is visible to the witness.

j. View the array, after completion, to ensure that the suspect does not unduly stand out.

k. Present each photo/individual to the witness one at a time, removing those previously shown.

l. Avoid saying anything or making any gestures to the witness that may influence the witness's selection.

m. If an identification is obtained, avoid reporting to the witness any information regarding the individual s/he has selected prior to obtaining the witness' statement of certainty.

n. Preserve the photos in their original condition.

2. Live Lineups: In composing a live lineup, the lineup administrator or investigator shall;

a. Include only one suspect in each identification procedure.

b. Select fillers who generally fit the witness' description of the perpetrator. When there is a limited/inadequate description of the perpetrator provided by the witness, or when the description of the perpetrator differs significantly from the appearance of the suspect, fillers should resemble the suspect in significant features.

c. Position the suspect randomly in each lineup, both across multiple cases and cases with multiple witnesses unless, the suspect or the suspect's attorney requests a particular position.

d. Include a minimum of four fillers (non-suspects) per live identification procedure.

e. Avoid reusing fillers in lineups shown to the same witness when showing a new suspect.

f. Consider that complete uniformity of features is not required or desirable.

g. Avoid using fillers who so closely resemble the suspect that a person familiar with the suspect might find it difficult to distinguish the suspect from the fillers.

h. Create a consistent appearance between the suspect and fillers with respect to any unique or unusual feature (e.g., scars, tattoos) used to describe the perpetrator by using images that cover those characteristics.

i. View the array, after completion, to ensure that the suspect does not unduly stand out.

j. Preserve the presentation of the lineup via videotape or by photographing the procedure.

B. **Conducting Lineups:** Presenting the photos/individuals by utilizing best practices ensures that the identification procedures minimize the chance of misidentification of a suspect. The method of preferred method of presenting the photos or individuals is the sequential, double blind method.

Double Blind Administration Procedures shall be employed by the Lineup Administrator to eliminate the possibility of influencing the witness' selection.

1. Sequential Photo/Live Lineup: When presenting the lineup, the administrator or investigator should provide instructions to the witness as follows:

a. Instruct the witness that he/she will be asked to view a group of photographs/individuals.

b. Instruct the witness that it is just as important to clear innocent persons from suspicion as to identify guilty parties.

c. Instruct the witness that the person who committed the crime may or may not be in the lineup being presented.

d. Assure the witness that regardless of whether an identification is made, the police will continue to investigate the incident.

e. Instruct the witness that the procedure requires the investigator to ask the witness to state, in his/her own words, how certain s/he is of any identification.

f. Instruct the witness that the photos/individuals will be viewed one at a time and that they are in random order.

g. Advise the witness to take as much time as needed in making a decision about each photo/individual before moving to the next one.

h. All photos/individuals will be shown, even if an identification is made.

i. If the witness requests to view the live lineup participants or photographs another time the individuals or images may be shown.
However, they will be shown in a new sequence. If the witness requests to view the individuals or photographs a third time the individuals or photos should be shown in a simultaneous manner. The witness requests for multiple viewing of the individuals or photos must be documented by the administrator.

j. Ensure that any identification actions (e.g., speaking, moving, etc.) are performed by all members of the lineup.

k. Instruct the witness not to discuss the identification procedure or its results with other witnesses involved in the case and discourage contact with the media.

l. Confirm that the witness understands the nature of the sequential procedure.

IV. Other Methods of Identification

A. The digital imaging system is composed of images taken during the booking process, the registration of a sex offender, or of an individual on a voluntary basis, or of a scanned photograph.

Viewing Preparations:

Ensure that positive identifying information is available for all individuals.

Ensure that the images are contemporary.

Ensure the showing of only one image of each individual during the viewing.

Select images by specific physical characteristics (e.g., race, age, sex).

Witness Instructions:

Instruct the witness without other persons present.

Describe the system to the witness only as a collection of images.

Instruct the witness that the person who committed the crime may or may not be present in the system.

Consider suggesting to the witness to think back to the event and his/her frame of mind at the time.

Instruct the witness to select an image if s/he can and to state how s/he knows the person.

Assure the witness that regardless of whether s/he makes an identification, the police will continue to investigate the case.

Instruct the witness that the procedure requires the investigator to ask the witness to state, in his/her own words, how certain s/he is of any identification.

Instruct the witness not to discuss the identification procedure or its results with other witnesses involved in the case, and discourage contact with the media.

B. **Composites Sketches**: A composite drawing is a specialized tool that may be utilized under conditions outlined in Policy O-406 entitled Police Sketch Artist.

C. **Show-ups:** The investigator should:

Determine and document the description of the perpetrator prior to the show-up.

Consider transporting the witness to the location of the detained suspect to limit the legal impact of the suspect's detention and crime scene contamination.

When multiple witnesses are involved, separate witnesses and instruct them to avoid discussing details of the incident with other witnesses.

If a positive identification is obtained from one witness, consider using other identification procedures (e.g., lineup, photo array) for remaining witnesses.

Caution the witness that the person s/he is looking at may or may not be the perpetrator.

Obtain and document a statement of certainty if identification is made.

All identifications and non-identifications must be documented.

V. Documenting the Results of Identification

A. The investigator shall preserve the outcome of the procedure by recording any identification results and witness's statement of certainty as follows :(**Note: EVERY Identification Procedure REQUIRES a supplemental report.**)

1. Document the date, time, names of all persons present and location of the procedure.

2. Document the procedure employed (e.g., sequential photo or live lineup, digital imaging system, etc.) in writing.

3. Document the results of the procedure, including the witness's own words regarding how certain s/he is of any identification.

4. Document items used and preserve the procedures presented to the witness for future court presentation.

5. Record both identification and non-identification results in writing on the witness identification form, including the witness's own words regarding how sure s/he is.

6. Ensure that the results are signed and dated by the witness and that no materials indicating other witness identification results are visible.

7. Ensure that the witness does not write on or mark any materials that will be used in other identification procedures.

XYZ POLICE DEPARTMENT
Individual/Photo Sequence Form

Case #_____Date_____Time _____AM/PM

I have received _____photographs/images from (assigned investigator) _____.
          (Print Administrators Name)

I have numbered each photograph/image on the back and shown them sequentially in a random order as listed below.

Photo Number In Order	Shown Name of Individual	Photo Comment
_____	_____	_____
_____	_____	_____
_____	_____	_____
_____	_____	_____
_____	_____	_____
_____	_____	_____
_____	_____	_____
_____	_____	_____

_____
(Witness Signature)

_____
(Administering Officer's Signature & Personnel #)

XYZ POLICE DEPARTMENT
Photo or Live Lineup Identification Instructions

Case # _____   Date _____ Time____AM/PM Location

I, _____, have been assigned
to (Administrator's Name Printed) administer this lineup to you.

I will advise you of the procedures for viewing the following lineup.

The fact that these photographs or individuals are being shown to you should not cause you to believe or guess that the guilty person (s) has been identified or arrested.

The person who committed the crime may or may not be in this lineup.

Regardless of whether you make an identification, the police will continue to investigate this incident.

It is just as important to clear innocent persons from suspicion, as it is to identify the guilty parties.

You will be shown a number of photographs/individuals one at a time before moving to the next.

All of the photographs/images will be shown even if an identification is made. If you recognize anyone, please wait until the procedure has ended before saying anything.

If you make an identification, please indicate in your own words how certain you are of the identification.

I have no additional information regarding this investigation.

Do not indicate in any way to other witnesses or other persons that you have or have not made an identification.

134

I, _____ understand the
          (Witness's Signature)
above information.

After viewing ___ photographs/persons, I have identified
photograph/individual _____ (#1, #2, etc.) photograph as that
of

_____
_____
_____.

Signed: _____
          (Witness's Signature)

Chapter 15
Implementing Eyewitness
Evidence Change

Change is never easy. It seems to be especially difficult within the law enforcement environment where we often hear statements like "There's no reason for it, its just department policy" or "We've never done it that way, we do it this way"! However, as we approach three hundred overturned criminal convictions based mainly due to mistaken eyewitness identifications, we believe that the time is long past overdue to change (modify) the way we conduct our eyewitness identification procedures.

The first step toward implementing change is to recognize that a problem exists with the procedures that your agency or department employ in cases with eyewitnesses. While we agree that the great majority of criminal cases with eyewitness identifications are handled properly and the witnesses make correct ID's, we have shown throughout this publication that a problem exists throughout the criminal justice system. Let us add that if there is sufficient corroborating evidence and your investigation has lead you the guilty party, it doesn't really matter what type of identification procedure is employed.[82]

Once you decide that a problem with eyewitness evidence exists, we suggest considering reviewing available research on the issues. We believe that you will need as much information as

---

[82] Paraphrased from statement of Professor Gary Wells, PhD, at the Baltimore County Police Academy, September 2000.

possible when you attempt to introduce a new policy to your department.

Then you create an identification policy, which is the basis or a guideline for the rank and file department members to implement when dealing with an eyewitness identification event. The initial writing or drafting of the policy should not be intimidating. There are a number of policies written and implemented by departments across the country that may be used and, if necessary, adjusted to fit your agency. One simple way is to start with adopting the Department of Justice's, *Eyewitness Evidence: A Guide for Law Enforcement*. This document provides the procedures for show-ups, simultaneous and sequential methods for live lineups and photo arrays. The Guide mentions the double blind administration but does not include the procedural guidelines. You are free to use the sample eyewitness evidence policy we have provided in the chapter on forms and operational orders. Other good sources of sample policy, training and procedures are available on the internet from the Municipal Police Institute and the Georgia Peace Officer Standards and Training Council.[83]

In the current economy all law enforcement administrators and District Attorneys have a concern of the cost of making policy changes, such as implementation and the training involved. We would be remiss not to mention that there have been a number of civil rights law suits won by those wrongfully convicted.

As a result of those settlements, cities and towns have paid tens of thousands and in some cases millions of dollars over the past several years to those wrongfully convicted. The cost of not having a contemporary written policy and what is more important is proper training in the area of eyewitness identification can be very expensive financially and, more importantly, with public trust.

There will be some minimal training costs involving the initial implementation, either as a full departmental training program, field training program or state academy; preferably all of those

---

[83] Available at www.mpitraining.com and www.gapost.org/ eyewitness_training.html

mentioned. A secondary issue of costs was that of court cost. What will cost the agency to schedule another officer, additional court overtime pay, for the cases that involve the blind administrator to testify? At the Northampton, Massachusetts Police Department Captain Patenaude found in his experience that in almost every case, the blind administrator was not subpoenaed to testify or, for that matter, to attend the court proceedings.

After all, what can the blind administrator testify to? We imagine the testimony would go something like this: "Officer, did you conduct the identification procedure in this case?" "Yes, sir, I did." "And officer, can you tell me about the facts of the case? "No sir, I can't." "Why is that?" "My only duty concerning this case was to conduct the lineup." "Officer, did you prepare a report regarding your participation or duties in this case?" "Yes, sir, I did." "Is this your report?" "Yes, sir, it is?"

Once the identification policy is drafted it should be scrutinized and accepted by the department's administration and, depending on jurisdictional requirements, the local district attorney. The next step in the process is for the department to make the decision as to which personnel within the agency will receive the training. We cannot state this enough; education is the key to any new policy because those responsible for carrying out the new procedures should, first, know why there is a need for this new policy and two, know how these procedures should be properly employed. The education should be agency wide, including the prosecutor's, so that everyone has a good working knowledge of the new procedures as they are stated in the policy. When the entire agency understands the identification policy this will be helpful in the future when an investigator is looking for a blind administrator. There should be someone within the agency that is both, unfamiliar with the identity of the suspect at the time of the identification procedure and is capable of providing testimony if called upon. A good start for training purposes is the Justice Department publication, *Eyewitness Evidence: A Trainer's Guide for Law Enforcement.* The publication is a lesson plan, complete with a

PowerPoint presentation, that explains why the changes in eyewitness evidence are necessary.

A good way to challenge whether the practitioners understand the new policy is to quiz them on the procedures presented to them during the training portion. This training program should become part of the department's field training program.

When the training has been completed and the agency is confident that the officers are ready to carry out the identification procedures the policy can be instituted/initiated with someone monitoring its progress, preferably a supervisor with some investigative experience. Any difficulties of carrying out a new policy should be discussed at bureau and staff meetings to determine if changes need to be made to improve the process. We strongly suggest you have regular conversations with the district attorney's office or your department legal advisor for input. This way everyone is on the same page and has the responsibility and ownership of conducting fair identification procedures from the onset.

It is also possible for a unit supervisor to develop and initiate eyewitness evidence change. The procedures advocated in this publication are legal and ethical. They do not violate the constitutional rights of suspects and are designed for use in cases with the least amount of corroborative physical evidence. We are aware of one state police investigative unit adopting sequential, double blind procedures, even though the agency itself had not formally accepted the procedures.

We strongly suggest that before any new eyewitness evidence identification policy being instituted, a statistical review of current eyewitness evidence cases be conducted for comparison with results from the new policy. We understand that many variables exist from case to case, week to week, etc., and that it is not possible to control the number of cases with eyewitnesses. We believe that a statistical review of eyewitness evidence cases over time would prove enlightening.

One last point, when then Lieutenant Patenaude, the Northampton, Massachusetts Detective Bureau Commander instituted a voluntary pilot program allowing the detectives themselves to choose between the standard simultaneous procedures and the new sequential double blind eyewitness procedures, he noticed that his personnel were using the new procedures exclusively. When he asked the detectives why they had switched procedures, the detectives responded that they felt much more confident and comfortable with the identifications they were obtaining from their witnesses, as well as understanding that the sequential double blind procedures may reduce the chance of a misidentification and/or wrongful conviction.

Chapter 16
Conclusions/The Future

The importance of adopting the eyewitness identification reforms cannot be overstated. The reforms bring uniformity and direction into a policy of reform for law enforcement across the country. These reforms improve a defective and antiquated eyewitness identification system in a simple cost effective manner that will assist in preventing further dual injustices. After all isn't our criminal justice system about putting the right person in prison for these serious crimes? Justice is not what we hope to achieve but what we are expected to achieve!

We also feel strongly that eyewitness evidence, like other forms of evidence, is only one part of a complete criminal investigation. During our lectures, we often refer to the triangle form of investigation. That investigative strategy states that every piece of evidence should, ideally, corroborate each other. So an identification of a suspect should corroborate a confession, which corroborates physical evidence, which corroborates the identification.

We believe that the problems associated with obtaining an identification tests that limits of an investigator's imagination. It is when faced with special circumstances, such as a suspect with tattoos, scars, missing fingers or strange appearances that the best investigators shine. It is then that we separate the merely good detectives from the truly excellent detectives.

Eyewitness identifications carry an enormous amount of weight in every legal proceeding. As the U.S. Supreme Court stated in *Watkins V. Sowders*, there is almost nothing more convincing than a live human being who takes the stand, points a finger at the defendant and says, "That's the one!"[84]

Law enforcement supervisors must be more aware of their role as a mentor and trainer to the personnel under their supervision. These supervisors must keep up with their subordinate's investigations as well as the new scientific trends and research relative to criminal investigations. This implies that supplemental reports are submitted in a timely manner, contemporary to the progress of the investigation.

Social Science research has been extensively conducted and the results published in the area of eyewitness evidence and human memory since the 1970s.

We sincerely hope that the future brings not only more research in eyewitness evidence and human memory, but also expose their published findings in various police periodicals where it will be easily accessible to criminal justice professionals.

We understand that scientific research must be published in scientific journals for peer review. We wonder, however, why there has not been (until recently) an attempt to disseminate the research results to law enforcement? Why aren't the results of the research submitted to the professional law enforcement magazines for review by law enforcement? While we understand that one study alone may not definitive, and that the researchers themselves agree, shouldn't the researchers share the results of their clinical research with the criminal justice professions when there is a scientific consensus among them?

We maintain that, while the research community has done extensive clinical tests, they remain somewhat blind to the legal and field constraints that law enforcement must operate under. Their research has been, to date, informative, definitive and eye

---

[84] See *Watkins v. Sowders*, 449 U.S. 341, 352 (1981)
[84] Indeed, some research goes back to, at least, 1932 when Edwin M. Borchard, a Yale Law School Professor, compiled a list of wrongfully convicted persons, most of which were due to faulty eyewitness identifications. In the publication he authored, Convicting the Innocent: Sixty-Five Actual Errors of Criminal Justice, he noted that mistaken identifications were practically alone responsible for

opening. We believe that the researchers, however, need to be exposed to actual field conditions. This means spending a significant amount of time patrolling with police officers and detectives so that they may observe field identification problems and talk with law enforcement officers about their procedures and views.

After observing the problems law enforcement faces each day, we then ask that these research professionals study the confirmation identification process employed in many large jurisdictions to obtain probable cause. We ask the research community to walk in our shoes and share our concerns for both the victim and the suspect.

As we have noted in this publication, many changes have been made, although slowly, in the way that law enforcement handles identification issues. More agencies everyday are either changing their policies or are developing eyewitness evidence policies. Following behind individual law enforcement agencies, several states have either legislated eyewitness evidence reforms or are examining ways to bring about change. We were happy to note that recently a newspaper reported that a shooting case in Riverview, Florida, handled by the Hillsborough County Sheriff's Department, was resolved after the suspect was selected from a *sequential* lineup as the shooter.[85] We also reluctantly admit that many law enforcement officers have not yet even heard of eyewitness identification guidelines. While reviewing appellate court decisions we found testimony from as recent as 2007 where a detective with thirteen years of experience in a large New England city testified that he "learned identification procedures through on the job training with seasoned officers and was not aware of any written procedures that his agency had for the administration of photographic arrays and he was not familiar with eyewitness identification procedures recommended by the United States

---

[85] Arrest made in fatal shooting at party St. Petersburg Times, Page 3B, August 1, 2011

Department of Justice its publication *Eyewitness Evidence, a Guide for Law Enforcement".* [86]

The National District Attorneys Association (NDAA) came out against any changes to eyewitness identification procedures during the time that the original Department of Justice, National Institute of Justice Technical Working Group was doing its work on the training guide.[87] While we cannot speak for the entire NDAA or its members, it appears that they, or at least some of their members are now in favor of the recommendations proposed in the Justice Department's Eyewitness Evidence Guide and subsequently published training manual.

In August of 2010, the New York State District Attorney's Association, through its best practices committee developed guidelines for photo and live lineups. The guidelines were formulated with the input of New York City Police department, the New York State Association of Chiefs of Police and the New York State Sheriff's Association and other law enforcement agencies.

Assistant State's Attorney Winn Collins from Wisconsin has written and published several papers on the benefits of the new eyewitness identification procedures. The Suffolk County, Massachusetts District Attorney has not only embraced the proposed changes, that office has been conducting training for local law enforcement agencies in their area. The U.S. Attorney's Office for Washington, D.C. wanted the D.C. Metropolitan Police Department to begin using double blind identification procedures when the police were changing their eyewitness evidence policy. The Department of Justice brought us and Professor Gary Wells to Washington, D.C. in December of 2004 in an attempt to bolster its position on identification issues with the Metro Police.

Sgt. Carroll was invited to lecture in Monroeville, Pennsylvania on October 23, 2006, when the Pennsylvania District

---

[86] See *Commonwealth v. Brandon Watson* SJC-10363 (Massachusetts, 2009)

[87] Letter from Kevin P. Meenan, President of the NDAA, to N.I.J. Director Sarah V. Hart , NIJ dated March 18, 2002.

Attorney's Association hosted a seminar for local law enforcement agencies on proposed changes to eyewitness identification procedures. These are just some of the examples of, what we believe is, a change of heart and philosophy on the part of prosecutors around the country.

Recently, the state of Florida, through its Innocence Commission, recommended the procedures described in *Eyewitness Evidence, a Guide for Law Enforcement.* The commission probably would have gone further to recommend additional steps for eyewitness identification, except for the objections of law enforcement. The state's major professional law enforcement associations fought tooth and nail against the reforms.

We feel that the citizens of Florida would have been better served had the commission followed the example of the Hillsborough County Sheriff's Department which mandates double-blind sequential identification procedures.

We maintain that if these law enforcement organizations would go to their memberships with a model policy, no reforms would be required at the state level. We believe that if law enforcement continues with it's, "We've never done it that way attitude," the legislatures of many states will codify identification procedures.

We still believe that legislation is not the way to improve eyewitness identification procedures. When we have testified to legislative bodies, we have stressed the importance for each law enforcement agency to develop a written contemporary policy for eyewitness evidence and that every officer be trained on the policy. Without the leeway to be innovative, many more cases will go unsolved, even when the actual suspect is known, because the facts of no two investigations are ever the same. Legislating investigative activity would severely limit law enforcement.

We are not the only voice suggesting law enforcement needs to change its procedures for collecting eyewitness evidence. In Massachusetts, the Supreme Judicial Court has endorsed the procedures recommended set forth in the Guide.[88]   Even the American Bar Association, Criminal Justice Section has recommended best practices for eyewitness identification procedures in an August 2004 resolution.

The Police Executive Research Forum (PERF) is currently conducting a nationwide survey of law enforcement agencies, using a Technical Assistance Group (TAG) of which Sgt. Carroll is a member, after being awarded U.S. Department of Justice grant funds, to learn the status of eyewitness evidence reforms. We hope that this study identifies where more effort should be made to change the way eyewitness evidence is obtained.

Software has been developed for use in photographic lineups. Early on, when departments converted to digital imaging with their identification photograph systems, law enforcement was forced to accept programs that were either not searchable or presented photos six or eight to a page, not single. However, we hope that when the new generations of software are developed, the programmers will contact law enforcement officers to ask what their needs are and what uses the software will have. This will help ensure that law enforcement will not be forced to adapt to the software. As stated earlier, live line ups can be demonstrated by using closed circuit monitors viewing each individual one at a time or when necessary this type of demonstration could be recorded and viewed by the witness at a later date.

The truth is this, if a police department takes the initiative to write a policy that institutes the sequential blind administration identification policy, train its' police officers on these new procedures to include the reason the changes are being made, and put the policy into practice then there are no excuses for the prosecutorial branch to dismiss or question the identification procedures as unacceptable. If the courts have accepted the procedures as best practices, and many law enforcement agencies across the country have accepted the sequential double blind

---

[88] *Commonwealth v. Silva-Santiago*, SJC-10154, 453 Mass 782; 906 N.E. 2nd, 2009

administration as best practices, then what reason could a prosecutor dismiss such a procedure as a part of their criminal case. With this in mind, what part of the sequential double blind administration of the eyewitness identification is unacceptable either technically or legally? It has been practiced for years without any significant issues other than the fact it reduces the chances of putting another innocent person in prison for a crime they did not commit while the guilty person is free to commit more crimes. In those few cases where a witness may not identify the guilty party because the procedure was sequential rather than simultaneous, couldn't that simply be a fact that the witness truly did not get a good enough look at the perpetrator to make an identification? We would rather our officers submit a witness identification based on a sequential blind administration than take a chance that the identification was a product of relative judgment from a simultaneous identification procedure resulting in a possible wrongful conviction.

It is interesting to note that a recent CBS Television show, The Good Wife (October 23, 2011), demonstrated a sequential live lineup which used a closed circuit monitor system for the witness to view. To our knowledge, this represents the first television portrayal of this type of identification procedure.

Biographies
Captain Kenneth Patenaude

Captain Ken Patenaude is a thirty-one year veteran of the Northampton, Massachusetts Police Department, retiring in January 2010. Captain Patenaude was a supervisor for over twenty-two years with eighteen years served in the detective bureau. Captain Patenaude holds a Bachelor's Degree in Law Enforcement and a Master's Degree in Criminal Justice Administration from Western New England University.

Captain Ken Patenaude has been recognized for his outstanding service as a member of the Department of Justice, Technical Working Group for Eyewitness Evidence. He played a key role in developing *Eyewitness Evidence; A Guide for Law Enforcement*, and to police departments on how to conduct criminal investigation interviews, show-ups, and lineups.

Captain Patenaude is a co-author of the eyewitness evidence instructional guide and training manual, and a published author of eyewitness evidence articles, and various departmental policies for the Northampton Police Department.

Captain Patenaude has lectured extensively on Eyewitness Evidence Procedures for numerous criminal justice agencies and organizations across the country. He has been invited to speak to a number of District Attorney's offices, Law Enforcement Agencies and Private Organizations, as well as Criminal Public Defense Attorney's. The topics have included Domestic Violence, Crime Scene Protection, and the Commonwealth's Firearms Laws.

Sergeant Paul Carroll

Sergeant Paul Carroll (retired) is a thirty-one year law enforcement veteran with over twenty-two year's detective division experience with the Chicago Police Department investigating and supervising investigations of homicides, suicides, suspicious deaths, sexual assaults and robberies. Sgt. Carroll was last assigned to the office of the Chief of Detectives as the Commanding Officer of the Crime Analysis Unit and aid to the Chief. He is a certified hostage negotiator and the author of numerous articles on crime scene protection and investigation, robbery and death investigations and the Chicago Police Department's policy for investigating domestic violence incidents and crime scene protection.

In addition, Sgt. Carroll is a consultant to numerous police departments, coroner's offices, prosecutors, public defenders, defense attorneys and the U.S. Department of Justice. He has traveled to El Salvador where he was a consultant to the Detective Division of the National Police (PNC) and lectured and consulted to the Independent Complaint Directorate (ICD) of the South African Police Service (SAPS), the agency charged with investigating high level government corruption, deaths in custody

150

or as a result of police action. Sgt. Carroll is currently a planning panel member of three Technical Working Groups for the National Institute of Justice (NIJ), Department of Justice and is a co-author of *Crime Scene Investigation*, a guide for law enforcement, *Eyewitness Evidence*, a guide for law enforcement along with its companion training guide and *Crime Scene Investigation*, a reference for law enforcement training. Sgt. Carroll is a frequent lecturer, having given hundreds of lectures over the last thirteen years at law schools, public defender's meetings, police departments and other venues within the country. He is an alumni and presenter at the Henry F. Williams/New York State Police annual Homicide Seminar and is a graduate of the 171st session of the prestigious FBI National Academy. Sgt. Carroll has appeared on America's Most Wanted, Dateline NBC, Court TV and the HBO America Undercover series.

Detailed resumes of the authors are available for review at www.paulbcarroll.com

Reference/Recommended Reading List

Edward Connors, Thomas Lundregan, Neil Miller and Tom McEwen, *Convicted by Juries Exonerated by Science: Case Studies in the Use of DNA Evidence to Establish Innocence After Trial*, available at: http://www.ncjrs.gov NCJ#: 161258

Eyewitness Evidence, A Guide for Law Enforcement, U.S. Department of Justice, National Institute of Justice, 1999, available at: http://www.ncjrs.gov/app/publications/abstract.aspx?ID'17824

Eyewitness Evidence, A Trainers Manual for Law Enforcement, U.S. Department of Justice, National Institute of Justice, 2003, available at: http://www.ncjrs.gov/app/publications/abstract.aspx?ID'188678

James M. Doyle, *True Witness*, , 2005, Palgrave MacMillan Publishing, New York, N.Y.

Garrett, Brandon L. *Convicting the Innocent-Where Criminal Prosecutions Go Wrong,* Harvard University Press, 2011

James M. Doyle, Esq. and Elizabeth F. Loftus, Ph.D , *Eyewitness Testimony, Civil & Criminal, 3rd Edition (and supplements).*, 1997, Lexus Law Publishing, Charlottesville, Va.

Gross, Jacoby, et al, *Exonerations in the United States, 1989 to 2003*, The Journal of Criminal Law and Criminology, Volume 95, No. 2, ,2005

Governors Commission of Capital Punishment, 2002, available at: http://www.idoc.state.il.us/ccp/ccp/reports/commission_report/summary_recommendations.pdf

152

Steblay, N., Dysart, J. & Wells, G.L. *Seventy-Two Tests of the Sequential Lineup Superiority Effect: A Meta-Analysis and Policy Discussion,* Psychology, Public Policy and Law, 17, 99-139, 2011

Adapting to New Eyewitness Identification Procedures (The Inside the Mind Series), 2010, Thomson Reuters/Aspatore

Truman Capote, *In Cold Blood*, 1965-First Vintage International, 1994

David Simon, *Homicide, A Year On The Killing Streets*, 1991, Houghton Mifflin Company

Ronald P. Fisher, Ph.D and R. Edward Geiselman, Ph.D *Memory-Enhancing Techniques for Investigative Interviewing, The Cognitive Interview,* 1992, Charles C. Thomas Publishing

Klobuchar, A., Steblay, N., & Caligiuri, H.L *Reforming Eyewitness Identification: Convicting the Guilty, Protecting the Innocent: Improving Eyewitness Identifications*: Hennepin County's Blind Sequential Pilot Project. Cardoza Public Law, Policy & Ethics Journal 4, 381-413.. 2006

Schacter, Daniel L, Dawes, Robyn, et al *Policy Forum: Studying Eyewitness Investigations in the Field.* Law and Human Behavior,. 2007
Wells, Gary L., Steblay, Nancy K., and Dysart, Jennifer E., *A Test of Simultaneous vs. Sequential Lineup Methods,* An Initial Report of the AJS National Eyewitness Identification Field Studies, American Judicature Society, 2011.

Rehm and Beatty, *Legal Consequences of Apologizing*, Journal of Dispute Resolution, Vol 1996, No 1, Pages 115-130,

Reevaluating Lineups, Why Witnesses Make Mistakes and How to Reduce the Chance of Misidentification (2009).

Wells, Gary L., *Eyewitness Identification: Systematic Reforms*, Wisconsin Law Review, Volume 2006, Number 2,

Schuster, Beth *Police Lineups: Making Eyewitness Identification More Reliable*, U.S. DOJ, NIJ Journal #258,

Using DNA Evidence to Exonerate the Innocent, available at: www.dna.gov/uses.postconviction

Eyewitness Evidence: Improving Its Probative Value, Psychological Science in the Public Interest, pgs 45-75. 2006

Turtle, John, Read, J. Don, Lindsay, D. Stephen, Brimacombe, C.A. Elizabeth, *Science of Eyewitness Evidence, Toward a More Psychological Science of Eyewitness Evidence,*. 2008

Cutler, B.L., & Penrod, S.D., *Mistaken Identification: The Eyewitness*, Psychology and the Law, Cambridge Press 1995.

Fisher, R.P. & McCauley, M.L *Information Retrieval: Interviewing Witnesses.*, Psychology & Policing 1995

Patenaude, Kenneth, *Improving Eyewitness Identification*, Law Enforcement Technology October, 2003.
Malpass, R.S. & Lindsay, R.L , *Measuring Lineup Fairness*, Applied Cognitive Psychology 13,. 1999.

James M Cronin, *Promoting Effective Homicide Investigations*, Community Oriented Policing Services, U.S. Department of Justice, , 2007.

Wells, Olson and Charman, *Distorted Retrospective Eyewitness Reports as Functions of Feedback and Delay*, Journal of Experimental Psychology, Vol.9, No. 1, pages 42-52. (2002)

Wells, Small, Penrod, Malpass, Fulero & Brimacombe, *Eyewitness Identification Procedures, Recommendations for Lineups and Photospreads*, Law and Human Behavior, 22, 603-647, (1998)

Two Cheers for the Department of Justice's Eyewitness Evidence: A Guide for Law Enforcement, Arkansas Law Review, 2000

Bradfield, Wells and Olson, *The Damaging Effect of Confirming Feedback on the Relation Between Eyewitness Certainty and Identification Accuracy,* Journal of Applied Psychology 87, pages 112-120 2002.

Collins, W., *.Improving Eyewitness Evidence Collection Procedures in Wisconsin*, Wisconsin Law Review Volume 2003, Number, pages 529-569,

Collins, W., *Looks Can Be Deceiving: Safeguards for Eyewitness Identification*, Wisconsin Lawyer, , March 2004.

Report of the Task Force on Eyewitness Evidence, District Attorney's Office, Suffolk County, Massachusetts, Fisher, 2004.

Getting it Right, Improving the Accuracy and Reliability of the Criminal Justice System in Massachusetts, Boston Bar Association Task Force, 2009.

Savage and Devendorf, *Conviction After Misidentification: Are Jury Instructions A Solution?,* The Champion (publication of the NACDL), , 2011

Brandon L. Garrett, *Convicting the Innocent: Where Criminal Prosecutions go Wrong*, Harvard University Press, 2011

Jim and Nancy Petro, *False Justice: Eight Myths that Convict the Innocent*, Kaplan Publishing, , 2011

McSweeney's, Eggers & Vollen, *Surviving Justice: America's Wrongly Convicted and Exonerated,* 2005

Westervelt and Humphreys, *Wrongly Convicted: Perspectives on Failed Justice,* Rutgers University Press, , 2001

Innocent: Inside Wrongful Conviction Cases, NYU Press, Scott Christianson, 2006

http://www.gapost.org/eyewitness_training.html

Schuster, *Police Lineups: Making Eyewitness Identification More Reliable*, NIJ Journal #258, available at: http://www.ncjrs.gov/app/publications/ncj219604

http://www.ncjrs.gov/app/publications/ncj208933

http://www.ncjrs.gov/app/publications/ncj208935

www.nlada.org/defender/forensics/for_lib/index/eyewitness%20id#eyewitness%20d

www.psychology.iastate.edu/faculty/gwells/homepage.htm

http://web.jjay.cuny.edu/~spenrod/penrod/

www.augsburg.edu/psychology/steblay.html

http://web.augsburg.edu/~steblay/improving_eyewitness_identification.pdf

http://eyewitness.utep.edu.bibliographies.html

www.fulero.com

www.nacdl.org/sl_docs.nsf/issues/eyewitnessid1

www.apls.org/links/publishingeyewitness.html

Selected Eyewitness Court Decisions

We frequently refer new detectives to appellate court decisions both to understand what the courts expect of law enforcement officers and for specific learning techniques.

In our opinion, we recommend that you refer to Manson V. Barithwaite, 42 U.S. 98, (1977), Neil V. Biggers, 409 U.S. 188, (1972) and U.S. v Wade, 388 U.S. 218, 228 (1967) and Kirby v. Illinois 406 U.S. 682 (1972) as the most often cited cases regarding eyewitness evidence issues.

The following cases (and those cases listed in the footnotes) contain issues relating to eyewitness identifications. The selected cases may not be binding or controlling in every jurisdiction.

We believe that a review of any (or all) of the listed cases will enhance the investigators knowledge of our courts' thinking. Some of the rulings may also bring a laugh or two or, at least a smile to your face.

State Appellate Court Cases

California v. Cook, 40 Cal. 4th 1334, 157 P.3d 950 (2007)
Commonwealth v. Botelho, 369 Mass. 860, 867 (1976)
Commonwealth v. Calhoun, 28 Mass. App. Ct. 949 (1990)
Commonwealth v. Clements, 436 Mass. 190 (2002)
Commonwealth v. Daye, 435 Mass. 463 (2001)
Commonwealth v. Ellis, 432 Mass. 746 (2000)
Commonwealth v. Florek, 48 Mass. App. Ct. 414 (2000)
Commonwealth v. Gomes, 453 Mass. 506, 507 (2009)
Commonwealth v. Horton, 434 Mass. 823 (2001)
Commonwealth v. Lieu, 50 Mass. App. Ct. 162 (2000)
Commonwealth v. Marrero, 436 Mass. 488 (2002)
Commonwealth v. Martin, 447 Mass. 274, 280 (2006)

Commonwealth v. Phillips, 452 Mass. 617, 628 (2008)

Commonwealth v. Pleas, 49 Mass. App. Ct. 321 (2000)

Commonwealth v. Poggi, 53 Mass. App. Ct 685 (2002)

Commonwealth v. Silva-Santiago, 453 Mass. 782, 795-796 (2009)

Commonwealth v. Tam 49 Mass. App. Ct. 31 (2000)

Commonwealth v. Vardinski, 53 Mass. App. Ct. 307 (2001)

Commonwealth v. Andre Walker, Mass. SJC 10470 (2011)

Commonwealth v. Ye, 52 Mass. App. Ct. 850 (2001)

Evans v. Texas, 643 S.W.2d 157; (1982)

Hemauer v. State, 64 Wis. 2d 62, 68, 218 N.W.2d, 342, 345 (1974)

Illinois v. Graham, 179 Ill. App. 3d 496, 534 N.E. 2d 1382 (1989)

Louisiana v. Holmes, 931 So. 2d 1157 (2006)

Nebraska v. Tolliver, 268 Neb. 920; 689 N.W.2d 567 (2004)

New Jersey v. Adams, 194 N.J. 186; A.2d 851 (2008)

New Jersey v. Herrera, 187 N.J. 493; a.2d 177 (2006)

North Carolina V. Tutt, 171 N.C. App. 518; 615 S.E.2d 688 (2005)

Penister v. State, 74 Wis. 2d 94, 246 N.W.2d 115 (1976)

People v. Corchado, 299 A.D. 2d 843, 749 N.Y.S. 814 (2002)

People v. Goodman, 109 Ill.App.3d 203, 64 Ill.Dec 793, 440 N.E. 2d 345(1982)

People v. Hartzel, 222 Ill.App.3d 631 (1991)

People v. Hines, 85 Ill. App. 3d 1047 (1980)

People v. Holiday, 47 Ill. 2d 300, 265 N.E.2d, 634 (1970)

People v. Johnson, 114 Ill. 2d 170 (1985)

People v. Kavanaugh, 85 Ill. 3d 783 (1980)

People v. Kubat, 94 Ill. 2d 437, 69 Ill. Dec 30 447 N.E. 2d 247 (1983)

People v. Laurenson, 131 Ill.App2d, 2 268 N.E. 3d 183 (1971)

People v. Miller, 254 Ill. App3d 997, 626 N.E. 2d 1350, (1993)

People v. Neal, 155 Ill.App.3d 340, 108 Ill.Dec 291, 295, 508 N.E. 2d 452, 456 (1987)

People v. Reid, 136, Ill.2d 27, 61 (1990)

People v. Rodgers, 3 Ill.App.3d 85, 279 N.E.2d 72 (1971)

People v. Rojas, 630 N.Y.S.2d 28, 36 (App. Div. 1995)

People v. Wolf & Kammes, 48 Ill.App.3d 736, 363 N.E. 2d 402 (1977)

People v. Wheeler, 71 Ill. App.3d 91, 27 Ill. Dec 235, 388 N.E.2d 1284 (1979)

Powell v. State, 86 Wis. 2d, 51, 271 N.W.2d 610 (1978)

Simos v. State, 83 Wis. 2d 251, 265 N.W.2d 278 (1978)

South Dakota v. Thunder, 272 N.W.2d 299; (1978)

State v. Avery, 213 Wis. 2d 228, 570 N.W.2d, 573 (1997)

State v. Dubose, 285 Wis.2d, 143 (2005)

State v. Lary R. Henderson, New Jersey (2011)

State v. Kaelin, 196 Wis. 2d 1, 538 N.W.2d 538 (1995)

State v. Ledbetter, 275 Conn. 534 (2005)

State v. Ledger, 175 Wis. 2d 116, 499 N.W.2d 198 (1993)

State v. McMorris, 213 Wis. 2d 156, 570 N.W. 2d 384 (1997)

State v. Outing, No. 17707 (Connecticut, 2010)

State v. Streich, 87 Wis. 2d 209, 274 N.W.2d 635 (1979)

State v. Waites, 158 Wis. 2d 376 462 N.W.2d 206 (1990)

State. V. Wolverton, 193 Wis. 2d 234, 533 N.W.2d 167 (1995)

State v. Wright, 46 Wis. 2d (1997)

Williams v. Alabama 354 So. 2d 48 (Al. 1977)

Williams v. Mississippi, 944 So. 2d 921 (2008)

Wisconsin v. Nawrocki, 308 Wis. 2d 227; 746 N.W. 2d 509 (2008)

Wright v. State, 46 Wis. 2d 75, 86, 175 N.W.2d 646, 652 (1970)

Federal Appellate & Supreme Court Cases

Amador v. Quarterman, 458 F.3d 397 (2006)
Biggers v. Tennessee, 390 U.S. 404 (1968)
Bratcher v. McCray, 419 F. Supp. 2d 352 (2006)
Colemn v. Quarterman, 456 F.3d 557 (2006)
Corchado v. Rabideau, 576 F. Supp. 2d 433 (2008)
Delaware v. Van Ardsall, 475 U.S. 673 (1996)
Foster v. California, 394 U.S. 440 (1969)
Gilbert v. California, 388 U.S. 263 (1967)
Gregory v. Louisville, et al, 444 F.3d 725 (2006)
Griffith v. Kentucky, 479 U.S. 314 (1987)
Guidry v. U.S., 546 U.S. 888, 126 S. Ct. 190, 163 L. Ed. 2d 198 (2005)
Holt v. U.S., 245 (1910)
Howard v. Bouchard, 405 F.2d 459 (2005)
Johnson v. Zerbst, 304 U.S. 458 (1938
Kirby v. Illinois, 406 U.S. 682 (1972)
Manson v. Braithwaite, 432 U.S. 98 (1977)
Millender v. Adams, 187 F. Supp. 2d 852 (2002)
Millerder v. Adams, 376 F.3d 520 (2004)
Moore v. Illinois, 434 U.S. 220 (1977)
Neil v. Biggers, 409 U.S. 198 (1972)
Ohio v. Roberts, 448 U.S. 56 (1980)
Perry v. New Hampshire (2011)
Simmons v. U.S., 390 U.S. 377 (1968)
Snow v. Sirmons, 474 F.3d 693 (2007)
State v. George, 645 N.W.2d, 777 (Nebraska 2002)
Stovall v. Denno, 388 U.S. 293 (1967)
U.S. v. Ash, 413 U.S. 300 (1973)
U.S. v. Brownlee, 454 F.3d 131 (2006)
U.S. v. Crews, 445 U.S. 463, 472 (1980)
U.S. v. Daily, 488 F.3d 796 (2007)
U.S. v. Fried, 6 Cir, 436 F.2d 784 (1971)

U.S. v. Garcia-Alvarez, 541 F.3d 8; (2008)

U.S. v. Garsson, 291 F. 646 (1923)

U.S. v. Guidry, 406 F.3d 314 (2005)

U.S. v. Maloney, 513 F.3d 350 (2008)

U.S. v. Montgomery, 100 F.3d, 1004 (1996)

U.S. v. Recendiz, 357 F.3d 511 (2009)

U.S. v. Rogers & Owens, 387 F.3d 925 (2004)

U.S. v. Saunders, 501 F.3d 384(2007)

U.S. v. Staples, 410 F.3d 484 (2005)

U.S. v. Wade, 388 U.S. 218 (1967)

Utley v. State, 826, S.W.2d, 268 (Arkansas 1992)

Young v. Sirmons, 486 F.3d 655 (2007)

Watkins v. Sowders, 449 U.S. 341, 352 (1981)

www.ingramcontent.com/pod-product-compliance
Lightning Source LLC
Chambersburg PA
CBHW071226290326
41931CB00037B/2010